D1172609

THE COMPLETE
BOOK OF
EGG COOKERY

Illustrations by

Lauren Jarrett

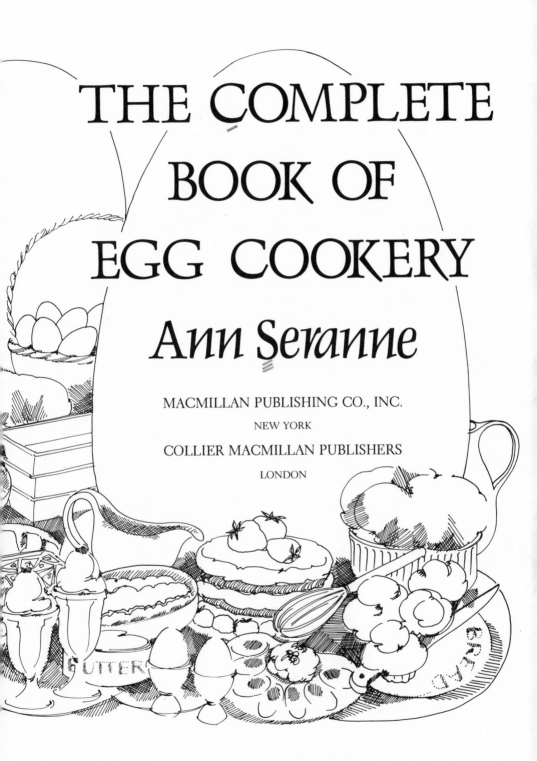

THE COMPLETE
BOOK OF
EGG COOKERY

Ann Seranne

MACMILLAN PUBLISHING CO., INC.

NEW YORK

COLLIER MACMILLAN PUBLISHERS

LONDON

Macmillan Publishing Co., Inc.
866 Third Avenue, New York, N.Y. 10022
Collier Macmillan Canada, Inc.
Library of Congress Cataloging in Publication Data
Seranne, Ann, 1914–
The complete book of egg cookery.
Includes index.
1. Cookery (Eggs)   I. Title.
TX745.S44   1983   641.6'75   82–18028

10 9 8 7 6 5 4 3 2 1

Printed in the United States of America

To Natalie and John—

a couple of good eggs

Contents

Introduction

Eggs play a most important role in all our cooking. First, they are essential in the construction of sauces, soufflés, custards, omelets and mousses. Second, eggs leven our cakes, meringues and frostings. Third, eggs emulsify our salad dressings and mayonnaise. Fourth, eggs bind our meat loaves and croquettes. Fifth, eggs clarify our consommés and bouillons. Sixth, eggs prevent crystallization in our ice creams, and, seventh, eggs are responsible for the crisp brown crusts achieved on fried foods and the golden crusts on pastry. In sum, eggs are indispensable to any cook.

There are 1,001 different dishes in which eggs are an essential ingredient, but there are less than a dozen methods of actually cooking them. The first chapter of this book presents the latest and best methods. On the ensuing pages are many new and delicious recipes in which eggs are used in combination with other ingredients. I hope you will enjoy them, and I hope my answers to anticipated questions you may have will be solved by the following observations:

What does one do with leftover yolks and whites?

Never throw out leftover yolks or whites. Freeze them, as outlined here, or store them covered in the refrigerator and use within a few days. There are numerous ways in which to use leftovers. For instance, additional whites in a soufflé will never hurt, or an extra egg yolk will add richness to a soup or sauce.

To freeze egg whites: Pour them into freezer containers, label with the number of whites and the date. Or, freeze each white in an ice-cube tray. When solid, transfer the cubes to a freezer container.

To freeze yolks (or whole raw eggs): Add a pinch of salt or 1½ teaspoons (7 grams) of sugar to each four yolks or two whole eggs. This helps retard gelation in the yolk. Put in freezer containers, label with date, number and note whether they contain salt or sugar. The finished dish you make from them will be somewhat thicker than if made with fresh eggs.

To thaw: Place freezer container overnight in refrigerator or run under cold water. Use yolks or whole eggs as soon as thawed. Once thawed, whites will beat to better volume if allowed to sit at room temperature for about 30 minutes.

Eggs *cannot* be frozen in their shells.

Can eggs be cooked in a microwave oven?
Never cook eggs in the shell in a microwave oven. They will explode.

What causes custards and sauces to curdle?
The answer is too high a cooking temperature. As soon as tiny bubbles begin to appear around the edge of a mixture, remove saucepan from heat and continue to beat rapidly to reduce temperature. You may take the precaution of using a candy thermometer. As soon as temperature approaches 182° F. (85° C.) remove from heat.

What discolors hard-boiled egg yolks?
It's all the cook's fault! The eggs were cooked too long or not cooled rapidly after cooking. The unattractive greenish color comes from sulphur and iron compounds in the egg, but the egg is still edible.

How can one distinguish a cooked egg from a raw egg?
To tell the difference between a hard-boiled egg and a raw egg, spin the egg on its side. The hard-boiled one will spin like a top. The raw egg will wobble and not spin.

Any difference between white and brown shells?
The color of the eggshell is determined by the breed of hens and has nothing to do with flavor, freshness or quality.

What is the best way to store eggs?
Buy refrigerated eggs and store them in the refrigerator as soon as you get home. However, even under refrigeration, eggs slowly lose carbon dioxide, which enlarges the size of the air cell and causes the yolk to flatten and the white to spread.

Why do some eggs have cloudy whites?

Cloudy whites are noticeable in freshly laid eggs. Cloudiness is an indication that the carbon dioxide, present in fresh eggs, has not yet escaped as a gas through the shell. As gas escapes, the white becomes clearer.

How can one tell when sugar is dissolved in meringue?

When beating sugar into egg whites in making meringue, rub a bit of the meringue between thumb and forefinger to test if sugar is dissolved. If it is not, mixture will feel grainy and you should continue to beat in the sugar.

What do certain egg terms mean?

Lightly beaten: Use a fork or whisk to beat eggs just until yolks and whites are blended.

Well beaten: Use an electric mixer or rotary beater and beat eggs until light, frothy and well blended.

Stiff, but not dry: Beat whites with a mixer or whisk until they no longer slip when the bowl is tipped but are still glossy looking. They should stand in soft peaks. If overbeaten, they will be difficult to blend into other foods and the finished product can be dry.

Beating egg whites: Whites beat to greater volume if at room temperature. A stabilizing agent, such as a pinch of cream of tartar or a squeeze of lemon juice, makes egg whites more stable.

Adding sugar to whites: Sugar also increases the volume and stability of beaten egg whites, but it must be added slowly, a couple of spoonfuls at a time. If added too quickly, sugar can decrease the volume.

Folding: When combining whites with heavier mixtures, they must be handled carefully or the air beaten into the whites is lost. The best method is to first stir in about one-quarter of the egg whites. This thins the basic mixture so that the balance of the egg whites can be incorporated more easily. Use a large metal spoon and a down, under and up motion.

What about the cholesterol question?

There has been a good deal of discussion about eggs and cholesterol. I do not propose that the reader eat soufflé or cream puffs every day. I would like to point out that many desserts, such as soufflés, are prepared with a number of eggs, but the equivalency is generally no more than one egg per serving and often less than that.

What size eggs are used in this book?

Although ingredients are specified in this book in both U.S. and metric measurements, an egg is an egg! All eggs used in the recipes are *large* size.

My thanks to the American Egg Board for so graciously sending me all the latest, pertinent information about eggs.

Ann Seranne

THE COMPLETE
BOOK OF
EGG COOKERY

I

The Basics
of Egg Cookery

In order to prepare your breakfast eggs or eggs for any of the vast number of dishes that follow, you will need to have the basic methods of cooking at your fingertips. This chapter will introduce you to a variety of methods and then you can select the ones you enjoy most.

Soft-Boiled Eggs

In my opinion, there is nothing better in the world of food than a perfectly soft-boiled fresh egg. But, if cooked too long or at too high a temperature, the egg quickly loses its epicurean qualities. The white becomes rubbery, the yolk develops an unattractive greenish-grey layer around the outer surface, and the entire egg becomes thoroughly indigestible.

Don't try to soft-boil eggs by instinct. They need precision timing. Keep a clock with a second hand on it in the kitchen and keep an eye on it, or buy one of those hypnotizing egg-timing gadgets that you turn upside down.

There are two methods by which you can soft-boil eggs. Method No. 1 gives me more consistent results. However, eggs cooked according to Method No. 2 are less apt to crack. Try both methods and you be the judge.

Method No. 1: Remove eggs from refrigerator and place them in a bowl of lukewarm water.

Fill a saucepan with enough water to come at least 1 inch (2.5 centimeters) above the eggs and bring water to a rapid boil.

Cook no more than two or three eggs at one time. Place eggs on a slotted spoon and slip gently into the rapidly boiling water. The eggs will reduce the temperature of the water to a simmer.

Reduce heat to keep water just at a simmer and cook eggs for 3 to 5 minutes, depending on the degree of doneness desired. At the end of 3½ minutes, the white of a large egg will be almost set and the yolk will still be runny. If the egg is exceptionally large, add one-half minute to the time; if the egg is exceptionally small, subtract one-half minute from the time.

Remove egg or eggs with slotted spoon and immediately run cold water over them until cool enough to handle and to prevent further cooking.

To serve: Break shell through middle with a knife. With a teaspoon, scoop egg out of each half shell into individual serving dish. If an eggcup is used, slice off large end of egg with a knife and enjoy egg from the shell. Sprinkle with a little salt and pepper and add a dab of butter, if desired.

Method No. 2: Put eggs in a single layer in a saucepan. Add enough cool water to come at least 1 inch (2.5 centimeters) above eggs and place over burner. When water begins to boil, turn off heat. If necessary, remove pan from burner to prevent further boiling. Cover saucepan and let eggs stand covered in the hot water for 2 to 4 minutes, depending on the desired doneness. Immediately run cold water over eggs until cool enough to handle. Serve as above.

Note: If necessary to keep a soft-cooked egg for a few minutes, drop it into a bowl of tepid water.

Hard-Boiled Eggs

There are two methods by which you can hard-boil eggs, and it is up to the cook to decide which he or she prefers. Piercing the large end of an egg with an egg piercer or thumbtack helps prevent eggs from cracking and leaking by providing an outlet for air pressure that has built up during the boiling process. But it is no guarantee. Piercing the end does, however, make shelling easier because the small amount of water that may seep in during boiling helps to separate the egg from the shell.

If eggs are especially fresh, they may be difficult to shell. Try placing cooled hard-boiled eggs in the freezer for 30 minutes. Set your egg timer and don't forget them. Then dip them in warm water and peel. The rapid expansion of the freezer-cold eggshell when it comes in contact with the warm water pulls the shell away from the egg.

Method No. 1: Place cold eggs in a bowl of lukewarm water to minimize shells cracking.

Bring water in a saucepan to a rapid boil, using enough water to come at least 1 inch (2.5 centimeters) above eggs.

With a slotted spoon transfer eggs to the boiling water. Reduce heat to keep water barely simmering and cook 12 minutes for large eggs. Adjust time about 2 minutes up or down for each size larger or smaller.

Drain eggs immediately and cover with cold water. Change water several times, if necessary, to cool eggs as quickly as possible and to prevent a dark surface from forming around yolks. (See page 10 for explanation.)

Method No. 2: Place eggs directly into a saucepan large enough to hold them in one layer and cover by at least 1 inch (2.5 centimeters) with cool water.

Bring water rapidly to a boil. Immediately turn off heat to prevent further boiling. Cover saucepan and let eggs stand in the hot water for 15 minutes for large eggs. Adjust time up or down by about 3 minutes for each size larger or smaller. Drain immediately and cover with cold water. Change water several times, if necessary, to cool eggs as quickly as possible.

To remove shells: Crack shells by gently tapping eggs all over, shattering the shells into many tiny pieces. Roll eggs between palms of hands to loosen shells, then peel, starting at the large end. Hold eggs under cold water or dip frequently into a bowl of cool water while removing the shells.

To serve: You'll meet hard-boiled eggs many times throughout this book in many guises—as hors d'oeuvres, in first courses, in luncheon and supper dishes, in sauces, in special breakfasts and in buffet dishes. Once cooked and cooled they may be refrigerated with or without the shell. If shelled, they should be sealed in a plastic bag and stored in a container with a lid to prevent the surfaces from drying.

Scrambled Eggs

There is no more delicious dish than perfectly scrambled eggs. To be perfect, they need strict supervision and must be cooked slowly until cooked through but still moist and creamy. If you don't want to devote your time to scrambling eggs, use the double boiler method. Scrambled in this fashion, they are called Rumbled Eggs and cook practically unattended. They may be kept waiting, also, for a short time before they are served.

REGULAR SCRAMBLED EGGS

4 eggs   2 tablespoons (30 grams) butter
Salt and white pepper   Chopped parsley or chives, optional

Break eggs into a bowl and sprinkle with a tiny bit of salt and a dash of white pepper. Beat quickly, but lightly, with a fork or whisk until yolks and whites are just blended.

Melt butter in an 8-inch (20-centimeter) frying pan over moderate heat until just hot enough to sizzle a drop of water. Swirl pan so butter coats sides and bottom. Give one last beat to the eggs and pour them into the pan.

For creamy eggs: Stir gently and constantly with a wooden spoon, scraping bottom and sides of the pan to prevent any one portion from becoming overcooked, for 3 to 5 minutes.

For large curl scrambled eggs: Hold a pancake turner, bottom side up, and draw it gently but completely across the bottom of the pan, letting the eggs form large curls. Continue until eggs are thickened but still moist, about 3 to 5 minutes.

Remove eggs immediately from heat and serve on warm—not hot—plates. Serves 2. If desired, top each serving with a dab of butter and sprinkle with a little chopped parsley or chives. The recipe may be doubled.

Caution: It is wise to remove scrambled eggs from the heat when slightly underdone because they will continue to cook from their own retained heat.

JIFFY SCRAMBLED EGGS

---

1 tablespoon (15 grams) butter   2 eggs

Heat butter in a 6-inch (15-centimeter) frying pan over medium high heat until just hot enough to sizzle a drop of water.

Break eggs directly into the pan. Immediately scramble with a fork. Stir continuously until eggs are thickened but still moist. Spoon directly onto a slice of hot buttered toast. Serves 1.

RUMBLED EGGS

---

1 tablespoon (15 grams) butter   Salt and pepper
4 eggs

For rumbled eggs, you will need a double boiler or a baking dish placed on top of a saucepan of boiling water. Put butter in the upper pan to melt. Meanwhile, beat eggs with a fork or whisk until yolks and whites are just blended. Beat in a little salt and pepper. Pour eggs into the hot butter and stir for a few seconds.

Place the eggs over gently bubbling water, giving them an occasional stir as you pass the stove. As soon as the eggs reach a thick, creamy consistency, remove double boiler from the heat, and the eggs will keep warm over the hot water until you are ready to serve. Serves 2 but recipe may be doubled.

No matter which method you choose to scramble eggs, they are particularly appetizing when served with crisply cooked bacon slices or browned sausage patties or sautéed chicken livers. Try scrambled eggs, also, served on slices of sautéed eggplant or aubergine or green tomato or in sautéed mushroom caps. Or try. . . .

SCRAMBLED EGGS WITH CROUTONS

Sauté small cubes of bread in butter until golden. Mix half into partially scrambled eggs and finish scrambling. Sprinkle remaining croutons over each serving.

SCRAMBLED EGGS WITH CHEESE

Add ½ cup (60 grams) of finely diced Swiss or Cheddar cheese to 6 eggs just before they begin to thicken.

SCRAMBLED CURRIED EGGS

Add a good dash of curry powder to the hot butter before scrambling eggs.

SCRAMBLED EGGS FINES HERBES

Scramble eggs with a little finely chopped parsley, tarragon and chives. Serve on hot buttered toast, dot with butter and sprinkle with any remaining herbs.

CREAMY SCRAMBLED EGGS

Mix ½ cup (125 grams) commercial sour cream and a dash of dry mustard into 6 beaten eggs before scrambling.

EGG TACOS

Scramble eggs and spoon into crisp taco shells. Drizzle on hot taco sauce, then sprinkle with cheese, lettuce and chopped tomato.

KANGAROOS

Halve a piece of Pita or pocket bread and open each half to form a pouch. Scramble eggs, adding chopped ripe olives, tomato and green pepper or capsicum to eggs as they begin to thicken. Tuck the eggs into the pockets and eat in your hand.

Poached Eggs

A perfectly poached egg, the yolk smoothly pocketed in the white, is a gourmet delight in almost every country in the world.

Poaching means to cook an egg, out of its shell, in hot liquid. The liquid may be water, milk, cream, broth, tomato juice or wine. The important point to remember is that the liquid must never boil.

POACHED EGGS

Eggs for poaching should be strictly fresh. Allow one egg per person: two if appetites are larger. Break an egg—first into a cup or shallow dish—then slip it into a frying pan or shallow saucepan of simmering, salted water. Water should just cover the white. Repeat until all eggs are in the poaching pan. Do not try to cook more than four eggs at one time in the average size frying pan. The eggs will automatically lower the water temperature so the heat should be immediately increased until the water bubbles again or to about 185° F. (85° C.), the perfect simmering temperature to produce tender perfectly poached eggs.

The average time to poach an egg is about 3 minutes, but it is not necessary to watch the clock. Keep your eye on the egg itself. You can easily see when the white and yolk are set to the desired firmness. Lift with a slotted spoon.

Eggs may be poached ahead of time. Undercook them slightly and store them floating in cold water in an airtight container in the refrigerator. To serve for morning breakfast, just slip the partially cooked poached egg into boiling water for about 30 seconds and serve immediately.

Serve poached eggs on or with buttered toast, Grilled English Muffin halves (page 150), large Round Croutons (page 149), hot corn bread, hot baking powder biscuits or on top of a potato cake or a bed of cooked rice. Accompany with a slice of fried ham, a rasher of crisp bacon or some fried sausage patties. You might also try the following variation:

EGGS POACHED IN SAVORY MILK

2 cups (½ liter) hot milk
Pinch each of marjoram and thyme
1 small bay leaf
Pinch of mace
6 peppercorns
4 poached eggs (see preceding recipe)

3 tablespoons (18 grams) flour
3 tablespoons (45 grams) butter, softened to room temperature
1 tablespoon (15 milliliters) sherry
Parsley or watercress for garnish

In a saucepan combine milk, a pinch each of marjoram and thyme, a small bay leaf, a pinch of mace and 6 peppercorns. Bring milk to a simmer and continue to simmer for 15 minutes. Strain milk into a small fry pan or shallow saucepan. Poach eggs in the savory milk, following basic recipe. Remove with a slotted spoon to a warm plate.

Combine flour and 2 tablespoons (30 grams) of butter to make a smooth paste. Stir the paste into the hot seasoned milk bit by bit. Cook, stirring, for about 3 minutes or until sauce is lightly thickened. Swirl 1 tablespoon (15 grams) butter and 1 tablespoon of sherry into the sauce. Pour over poached eggs and garnish with parsley or watercress. Serves 2 or 4.

Fried Eggs

There are two good basic ways to fry eggs. Either way, eggs should be fried at a moderately low temperature so that the whites will not be toughened by too intense heat.

Method No. 1: Heat some butter or bacon fat—about 1 tablespoon (15 milliliters) fat for each two eggs—in a frying pan until hot enough to sizzle a drop of water.

Carefully break 2 eggs into a saucer or shallow dish and slip them into the frying pan.

Reduce heat immediately and cook over low heat, basting eggs with some of the hot fat until the white is no longer transparent and the yolks are set. If you want to brown the eggs on their other sides, flip them over for a few more seconds.

Season with salt and pepper and serve immediately.

Method No. 2: Use just enough butter to coat bottom of a frying pan lightly. Heat pan until butter is hot enough to sizzle a drop of water.

Break eggs into a saucer or shallow dish and slip gently into the pan. Reduce heat immediately and cook over low heat for about 1 minute, until edges turn white.

Add 1 teaspoon (5 milliliters) water for each egg and cover frying pan tightly to hold in steam, which will cook the eggs. Cook to desired degree of firmness.

Fried eggs are delicious served with pan-fried potatoes and almost any other cooked vegetables, such as slices of fried eggplant or aubergine and tomato. Broiled or grilled ham slices and pineapple are also nice accompaniments.

As I mentioned earlier, eggs should be fried at moderately low temperatures, but, there are, as in all rules, exceptions. You might like to try one just for the fun of it.

FRIED EGGS (South-of-France-style)

Olive oil is used extensively for frying in the South of France where this recipe originated. The egg is broken into a saucer, sprinkled with salt and pepper, and is then slid gently into a frying pan holding about 2 tablespoons (30 milliliters) of smoking oil. The frying pan is tipped and the egg is dropped into the place where the oil is deepest. With a wooden spoon, quickly curl the white of the egg around the yolk. This keeps the yolk soft and digestible and is the secret of the pretty white ruffle that forms around the egg.

Here are some other fried egg ideas you might like to try. . . .

FRIED EGGS BEURRE NOIR

Fry 4 eggs by either basic method and arrange on a warm serving platter. Add to the frying pan 4 tablespoons (60 grams) butter and cook over low heat until butter is a rich golden brown. Add 1 tablespoon (15 milliliters) wine vinegar, a little salt, and some coarsely ground pepper. Bring to a boil and pour over the eggs. A few chopped capers may also be added along with the vinegar, if desired. Serves 2 or 4.

EGG-IN-THE-HOLE

Cut 2½-inch (6-centimeter) rounds from the center of slices of trimmed bread; reserve the cut-out pieces. Melt some butter in a frying pan. I can't tell you just how much, but, when it has been absorbed by the bread, add some more. When the butter is foaming, place the slices of bread and the cut-outs in the frying pan. Quickly break an egg into the hole in the center of each slice. Cook for 1 minute on that side, turn both egg and toast and cook another minute or until eggs and bread are golden brown. Turn the cut-outs, also. Serve with a sautéed cut-out sitting on top of the egg. Serves 1. If desired, serve with chili sauce or taco sauce.

Baked or Shirred Eggs

For all practical purposes baked and shirred eggs can be considered one and the same method of egg cookery. The only difference is that baked eggs are cooked entirely in a preheated oven while shirred eggs are begun over direct heat and transferred to the preheated oven. In both cases the whites should be creamy and soft and the yolks should be barely set with just a film of transparent white over them.

Method No. 1: For each person to be served, butter a ramekin, shallow baking dish or 9½-ounce (285-gram) custard cup. Break and slip 2 eggs into the dish. Sprinkle lightly with salt and pepper. Spoon over the eggs 1 tablespoon (15 milliliters) light cream and dot with 1 teaspoon (5 grams) butter.

Bake in a preheated 350° F. (180° C.) oven for 15 minutes or until whites are set and yolks are soft and creamy. Serve immediately.

Method No. 2: For each person to be served, melt 1 tablespoon (5 grams) butter in an individual heatproof baking dish or ramekin over low heat. Do not let butter brown. When melted, slip 2 eggs into the dish and sprinkle lightly with salt and pepper. (For aesthetic reasons, many cooks like to omit the pepper as it marks the eggs.)

Pour 1 tablespoon (15 grams) hot melted butter over the egg yolks and transfer baking dish to a preheated 350° F. (180° C.) oven.

Bake for about 15 minutes, or until whites are milky but still creamy and the yolks are set to the desired degree. Serve immediately in the baking dish.

Note: If a 325° F. (170° C.) oven is a more convenient temperature for you, just add 5 to 8 minutes to the baking time.

Baking and shirring are excellent methods of preparing eggs for a crowd of people. Instead of small individual ramekins, try using tomato, pepper or capsicum cases or use large baking dishes. When the eggs are cooked in individual portions the dishes should be just large enough to hold two eggs plus some bacon, sausages or chicken livers. Here are some other recipe ideas. . . .

⬧

EGGS BAKED IN CREAM

For each person to be served, melt 1 teaspoon (5 grams) butter in an individual shallow heatproof baking dish. When butter is melted, slip in 2 eggs. Pour a little hot cream over the eggs and transfer to a preheated 325° F. (170° C.) oven for about 20 minutes, or until set to taste.

EGGS AU PLAT ANGLAIS

For each person to be served, cook 2 strips bacon until crisp and golden; drain on absorbent paper. Spoon 1 tablespoon (15 milliliters) of the bacon fat into an individual shallow heatproof baking dish and slip in 2 eggs. Cook for 1 minute over low heat, then tip dish and spoon a little of the hot bacon fat over the yolks. Transfer to a preheated 350° F. (180° C.) oven for about 15 minutes, or until set to taste.

EGGS BAKED WITH BREAD CRUMBS

For each person to be served, melt 1 teaspoon (5 grams) butter in bottom of an individual shallow heatproof baking dish. Tip dish to coat sides. Sprinkle bottom and sides with fine cracker or bread crumbs and sprinkle lightly with salt and pepper. Slip 2 eggs into the dish and cook for 1 minute over low heat. Transfer to a preheated 350° F. (180° C.) oven and bake for 15 minutes, or until set to taste.

BAKED EGGS IN TOMATO JUICE

Allow 2 eggs per person to be served. Butter a shallow heatproof baking dish large enough to hold the number of eggs you wish to cook in one layer. Fill the dish half full of hot, well-seasoned tomato juice. Slip eggs into the juice and cook for 2 to 3 minutes over direct heat until tomato juice begins to simmer. Sprinkle with salt and pepper to taste, chopped parsley or a favorite herb, and dot with butter. Transfer to a preheated 350° F. (180° C.) oven and bake for about 15 minutes, or until eggs are set to taste.

EGGS AU FOUR GRUYÈRE

Allow 1 or 2 eggs per person to be served, depending on appetites and how you plan to serve the eggs.

Cut slices of day-old bread and thin slices of Gruyère cheese into rounds of equal size and large enough to serve as a base for an egg.

Sauté bread rounds in butter, on one side only, until golden brown. Remove and place a round of cheese on the fried side.

Place bread rounds, cheese-side up, in a buttered baking dish in which they will be served and grind a little pepper over them. Break an egg on top of each round and dot with butter. Sprinkle with a little salt.

Bake in a preheated 325° F. (170° C.) oven for about 20 minutes, or until eggs are set to taste.

SHIRRED EGGS MORNAY

2 cups (½ liter) Light Cream Sauce
   (page 200)
2 egg yolks
¼ cup (30 grams) grated Parmesan
   cheese

¼ cup (30 grams) shredded Swiss or
   Gruyère cheese
6 eggs

Heat Light Cream Sauce and stir in the egg yolks after beating them with a little of the hot sauce. Stir in half the cheeses and cook, stirring until cheese is melted. Do not let sauce boil.

Pour a layer of this sauce into three well-buttered individual shallow baking dishes. Slip eggs into the sauce one at a time, using two eggs for each dish. Pour remaining sauce around edge of eggs, leaving yolks of eggs partially showing. Sprinkle with remaining cheese.

Bake in a preheated 375° F. (190° C.) oven for 12 to 15 minutes, or until eggs are set to taste. Serve in the baking dishes. Serves 3.

Eggs en Cocotte

Cocottes are small earthenware, china or silver saucepans with handles, deep enough to contain one egg and a couple of tablespoons of a savory addition, such as cooked vegetable puree, crumbled bacon, lobster meat or creamed chicken. This is known as the garniture. Small china ramekins or 6-ounce (180-gram) custard cups may be substituted for the cocottes.

Eggs cooked in this manner make delightful decorative dishes for a special breakfast or a breakfast tray and also make a dainty first course to a formal luncheon or dinner. Let's try here the basic egg en cocotte suitable for breakfast.

BREAKFAST EGG EN COCOTTE

Into each individual cocotte, ramekin or custard cup pour 1 tablespoon (15 milliliters) hot, heavy or thick cream. Break one egg at a time into a saucer and slip it into the dish on top of the cream. Sprinkle each egg with a little salt and pepper and dot with ½ teaspoon (2 grams) butter.

Set each cocotte into a saucepan or deep frying pan containing enough boiling water to reach to within ½ inch (1 centimeter) of the top of the dishes. Cover and cook over low heat or in a preheated 400° F. (200° C.) oven for 8 to 10 minutes or until the whites are just set and the yolks are set but still glossy.

Remove dishes from the water bath and dry their outsides before serving.

Eggs in Molds

Eggs may be poached in a variety of fancy molds, timbale molds or in just about any container that is the right size to hold one egg comfortably with a little garniture. They are cooked in the same way as Eggs en Cocotte, but with one difference, and that is the cooking time. The eggs are cooked for 12 to 15 minutes or until sufficiently set to allow them to be turned out upside down onto a sautéed Round Crouton (page 149) or other savory base. The base might be a bed of mashed potatoes or cooked vegetable puree, a broiled mushroom cap or tomato half, a cooked artichoke bottom, or an Individual Tart Shell (page 112). Eggs in molds usually are served with a rich gravy or cream sauce, and the bottoms of the molds are garnished with sliced truffle, a square of pâté or cooked vegetables. If the molds are so garnished, any sauce should be served separately. You don't want to mask a thing of beauty with a sauce.

Eggs Mollet

Another delicate method of cooking eggs is known as Eggs Mollet (pronounced *moe-lay*). They are cooked according to Method No. 1 for soft-boiled eggs but for a longer time period, yet not long enough to hard boil them. Mollet eggs, in fact, are a delicious compromise. They are frequently served cold in a sparkling aspic.

EGGS MOLLET

Follow Method No. 1, page 15, for Soft-Boiled Eggs, but cook them in simmering water for 5½ to 6 minutes for large eggs. Adjust time up or down about ½ minute for each size larger or smaller.

Immediately drain off hot water and cover eggs with cold water. Change water several times while the eggs are cooling to prevent further cooking. When thoroughly cool, remove shells—*very* gently!

Eggs Mollet may be prepared in advance. To reheat, place eggs in a saucepan and cover with very hot, but not boiling, water. Let stand for 5 minutes.

You may serve them in almost any way suitable for poached eggs. As many as a dozen may be cooked at the same time, making them an ideal dish for a crowd of hungry guests.

Coddled Eggs

Probably the most delicate method of cooking eggs in their shells is known as coddling.

Basic method: Transfer eggs from refrigerator to a bowl of lukewarm water. Fill a saucepan with enough water to come at least 1 inch (2.5 centimeters) above eggs. Bring water to a rapid boil.

Place eggs, 1 or 2 at a time, on a slotted spoon and slip them into the boiling water. Remove saucepan immediately from heat. Cover saucepan with a tight-fitting lid and let eggs cool in the water for 8 to 10 minutes, depending upon degree of doneness desired. The yolks in large eggs will be barely set and the whites will be creamy. Adjust time up or down about 1 minute for each size larger or smaller. Remove eggs from the water, cool, if necessary, and serve as you would a soft-boiled egg.

Baked Bacon

Because of its affinity to eggs, there is perhaps no better time in this book than right now to give you the recipe for perfect bacon. The following recipe produces crisp and golden bacon every time with a minimum of shrinkage, and it is particularly useful when cooking bacon for a group.

BAKED BACON

If possible, take bacon from the refrigerator 30 minutes before using. If not, place the cold slab of bacon in a hot oven (400° F., 200° C) for about 5 minutes to soften.

Separate slices from the slab and arrange side by side in aluminum broiling or grilling pans. The edges may overlap slightly. Bake in the preheated oven according to the following temperature chart. Drain on absorbent paper and keep warm until ready to serve.

Bacon Times and Temperatures

400° F. (200° C.) 15 minutes
350° F. (180° C.) 20 to 25 minutes
325° F. (170° C.) 30 minutes

2

Special Breakfast Ideas

The breakfast hour is a wonderful time of day. In this era of servantless households there is no one to prepare breakfast for me or bring a breakfast tray, but *me*. But I do enjoy asking friends for breakfast, which can mean nothing more than amusing chitchat, or we may use the hour to share problems and thoughts. For my houseguests, I enjoy serving breakfast in bed on trays unless they are violently opposed to it, and few are. In sum, breakfasts can be as special and rewarding as other meals that you may take hours planning.

Here are some ideas for weekend breakfast treats, surprise breakfast trays, breakfasts for guests, old-fashioned English breakfasts and hunt country breakfasts.

Weekend Breakfast Treats

Serve with hot buttered toast or a hot bread and piping hot, honest coffee or tea. Start with fresh fruit in season or juice freshly squeezed, if possible.

POACHED EGGS DIABLE

3 tablespoons (45 grams) butter
2 scallions or spring onions, minced
2 tablespoons (30 milliliters) wine
 vinegar
1 tablespoon (15 grams) prepared
 mustard, preferably Dijon
1 tablespoon (8 grams) chopped
 mixed herbs (parsley, chives, tarragon)

1 cup (¼ liter) Basic White Sauce
 (page 200)
1 egg yolk
2 tablespoons (30 milliliters) heavy or
 thick cream
4 Poached Eggs (page 21)
4 sautéed Round Croutons (page 149)

In a small saucepan melt 1 tablespoon (15 grams) butter and sauté onions until transparent.

Add vinegar, mustard, and herbs. Heat to simmering. Stir this mixture into the Béchamel.

Combine egg yolk with cream and a little of the hot Basic White Sauce, then stir into the remaining warmed Basic White Sauce and cook over very low heat, stirring constantly, while adding remaining 2 tablespoons butter bit by bit. Do not let sauce boil.

Arrange a Poached Egg on each crouton and spoon sauce over. Serves 2. Recipe may be doubled.

EGGS LANDAISE

1 tablespoon (15 grams) butter
1 medium onion, chopped
½ pound (250 grams) pork sausage in
 links or patties

2 tomatoes, peeled and chopped
4 eggs

Melt butter in a medium-sized frying pan and sauté onion in it until golden.

Add sausage and tomatoes and cook for 15 minutes, stirring occasionally.

Fry eggs (page 22) to desired degree of doneness.

Place tomato mixture onto serving plates and top each with a couple of fried eggs. Serve with hashed brown or pan-fried potatoes. Serves 2. You may double this recipe.

SWISS EGGS

2 tablespoons (30 grams) butter
4 eggs
4 thin slices Swiss cheese
6 tablespoons (90 milliliters) heavy or
    thick cream

Salt and freshly ground white pepper
    to taste

Melt butter in shallow heatproof baking dish large enough to hold the eggs. Slip eggs into the melted butter and cook over low heat for about 2 minutes.

Cover eggs with slices of cheese and pour cream over the cheese. Sprinkle with salt and pepper and bake in a preheated 325° F. (170° C.) oven for about 20 minutes, or until eggs are set to taste. Serves 2. Recipe may be doubled.

Variation: Crumble 4 strips crisp Baked Bacon (page 30) over eggs before covering them with the cheese.

EASY CREAMED EGGS

2 tablespoons (30 grams) butter
2 tablespoons (12 grams) flour
1 cup (¼ liter) hot milk
1 tablespoon (8 grams) chopped
    parsley
Dash of Worcestershire sauce

A few drops of Tabasco or a similar
    hot pepper sauce
Salt and pepper to taste
4 Hard-Boiled Eggs (page 16), shelled
    and sliced

In a small saucepan melt butter. Stir in flour and cook over moderate heat until mixture bubbles. Remove from heat.

Add hot milk and stir rapidly until mixture is blended. Return to heat and cook, stirring, for a few minutes, or until sauce is thickened. Cook over low heat for 10 minutes, stirring occasionally.

Mix in remaining ingredients. Heat for several minutes before serving. Serve on hot buttered toast or Grilled English Muffins (page 150). Serves 2.

Variation: Coat fresh ripe tomato slices on both sides with flour. Sauté quickly in butter until lightly browned. Place a slice of tomato on a Round Crouton (page 149) and cover generously with creamed eggs. Add a sprig of chopped parsley for color.

FRIED EGGS CATALANA

2 tablespoons (30 milliliters) vegetable oil

1 medium onion, chopped

2 ripe tomatoes, peeled and sliced

1 green pepper or capsicum, seeded and diced

¼ pound (125 grams) mushrooms, trimmed and sliced

Salt and freshly ground pepper to taste

4 eggs

In a medium-sized frying pan heat oil and sauté onion over moderate heat until golden. Add tomatoes, green pepper and mushrooms. Sprinkle with a little salt and freshly ground pepper and simmer for 20 minutes, until onions and pepper are soft.

Fry eggs by either method (page 22) to desired degree of firmness and transfer to a warm serving platter. Surround by a border of sautéed vegetables. Serves 2. Recipe may be doubled.

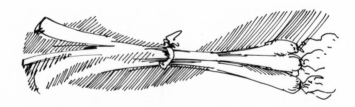

Surprise Breakfast Trays

An amusing incident occurred many years ago that might be appropriate to relate here. A delightful gentleman named André Simon was visiting from England. He was president of the English Wine and Food Society and a respected connoisseur of food. Each morning I trotted up the winding staircase with a handsomely appointed breakfast tray. It was always a hearty meal: scrambled eggs with ham or bacon or a broiled kipper, toast tucked between folds of a napkin, and tea especially brewed from an unusual blend. It was not until Mr. Simon was bidding farewell that I realized he was French, not English, and probably would have preferred a cup of café au lait and a croissant. I have often wondered how much of those bountiful breakfasts he ate and how much he fed to the birds!

But, back to breakfast trays: Use your prettiest china and, when possible, float a blossom in a crystal bowl or put a single flower in a bud vase on the tray. Keep the food dainty, colorful and appetizing.

With the following surprise egg dishes, popovers are a treat. Don't forget a pat of unsalted butter and a small dish of good marmalade or jam. Be sure to ask if guests prefer coffee or tea.

EGGS IN THE NEST

2 eggs
Pinch salt
2 tablespoons (30 grams) minced
    cooked ham

2 large sautéed Round Croutons (page 149)

Separate eggs, keeping each yolk whole in half an eggshell. Prop shells up against side of a dish.

In a medium-sized bowl beat egg whites to a stiff froth. Add salt and continue to beat until whites are stiff, but not dry. Fold in minced ham.

Pile egg whites on the Round Croutons on a baking sheet. Make a well in center of each. Slip a yolk into each well.

Bake in a preheated 350° F. (180° C.) for 12 to 15 minutes, or until yolks are cooked to the desired degree. Serves 1 or 2.

Variation: Spoon some Hollandaise Sauce (page 205) over the yolks before serving.

BAKED SCRAMBLED EGGS

2 eggs
1 tablespoon (15 milliliters) light
    cream

Mornay Sauce (page 200)

Butter a small cocotte or custard cup generously. Beat eggs and cream and pour into prepared dish. Place dish in a shallow pan containing 1 inch (2.5

centimeters) hot water and bake in a preheated 325° F. (170° C.) oven for 20 to 25 minutes, or until a knife inserted in center comes out clean.

Unmold onto a warm serving dish and cover with Mornay Sauce. Serves 1.

EGGS D'AURIA

1 toasted Croustade (page 150)	2 eggs
1 chicken liver, halved	Salt and pepper to taste
1 tablespoon (15 grams) butter	Chopped tarragon to taste

Keep Croustade warm in a low oven.

Sauté the chicken liver in a small saucepan in the butter until lightly browned and just cooked through. Set aside.

Beat eggs lightly and scramble in the butter remaining in pan. While still creamy, empty scrambled eggs into the croustade, place chicken liver on top and sprinkle with a little salt, pepper and the chopped tarragon. Serves 1.

BLUSHING EGGS

1 ripe red tomato	2 eggs, lightly beaten
Salt and pepper to taste	Parsley for garnish
1 tablespoon (15 grams) butter	

Cut tomato in half and scoop out seeds and centers, leaving two shallow cups. Be careful not to break through the skin. Place cut-side up on greased baking dish and sprinkle with salt and pepper. Dot with half the butter and bake in a preheated 400° F. (200° C.) oven for 5 to 6 minutes.

Meanwhile, chop soft pulpy flesh of the tomato and combine with the eggs. Melt remaining butter in a frying pan and in it scramble the egg-tomato mixture, stirring constantly, until thickened but still creamy.

Remove tomatoes from oven, transfer to serving plate, fill with scrambled egg and garnish each cup with a sprig of parsley. Serves 1.

EGGS MARCHIONESS

3 medium mushrooms, sliced	Salt and pepper
1 tablespoon (15 grams) butter	1 tablespoon (15 milliliters) heavy or
1 egg	thick cream

In small saucepan sauté mushrooms in half the butter until tender.

Spread mushrooms in bottom of a small baking dish or ramekin. Break the egg on top of mushroom mixture and sprinkle with a little salt and pepper. Dot egg with remaining butter and pour cream around side of dish.

Bake in a preheated 325° F. (170° C.) for 20 minutes, or until egg is set to taste. Serves 1.

OEUFS ADONIS

Place an Egg Mollet (page 29) or a Poached Egg (page 21) on a sautéed Round Crouton (page 149) in a heatproof shallow dish. Coat egg with Mornay Sauce (page 200) and sprinkle with grated Parmesan cheese mixed with an equal quantity of fine bread crumbs. Sprinkle with a little melted butter and brown six inches (15 centimeters) from broiler or grill heat until sauce is bubbling and tinged with brown. Serves 1.

EGG AND CHICKEN

Fill an Individual Tart Shell (page 112) with creamed chicken. Place an Egg Mollet or Poached Egg (pages 29 and 21) on top and cover with hot Medium Cream Sauce (page 199). Add parsley for garnish. Serves 1.

Breakfasts for Guests

Breakfast with guests offers a relaxing informal opportunity to catch up on gossip and events over slightly more opulent fare than you would normally serve to family. For that reason, the egg dishes that follow can be prepared almost entirely in advance with a minimum of last-minute fuss and frills.

BAKED STUFFED EGGS MORNAY

4 cups (1 liter) Mornay Sauce (page 200)
12 Hard-Boiled Eggs (page 16), shelled
6 tablespoons (90 grams) butter
½ pound (250 grams) mushrooms, minced

2 tablespoons (15 grams) chopped parsley
Crumbled dried tarragon to taste
1 cup or 2 slices (125 grams) fresh bread crumbs
2 tablespoons (15 grams) grated Parmesan cheese

Make Mornay Sauce and set aside, covered.

Cut eggs in half lengthwise. Empty yolks into a bowl; reserve whites.

Heat 4 tablespoons (60 grams) of the butter in a small frying pan. Sauté mushrooms for about 5 minutes, or until mixture is almost dry, stirring occasionally. Stir in parsley and tarragon.

Mash egg yolks with ½ cup (125 milliliters) of the Mornay Sauce. Stir in mushroom mixture and fill whites with the yolk mixture.

Spread a thin layer of Mornay Sauce in a shallow baking dish large enough to accommodate all the eggs in one layer, and arrange eggs in the sauce, stuffing-side up. Spoon remaining sauce over.

Melt remaining 2 tablespoons (30 grams) butter and toss with bread crumbs. Sprinkle over the eggs. Sprinkle with Parmesan cheese. Cool, cover and refrigerate until needed.

To serve: Bake in a moderate 350° F. (180° C.) oven for 30 to 35 minutes. Serves 6. Serve with hot Brioche (page 147) and strawberry jam. A wedge of melon with a twist of lime makes a refreshing first course.

EGGS CECELIA

---

6 tablespoons (90 grams) hot melted
    butter
3 ripe tomatoes, peeled and halved

6 eggs
Salt and pepper to taste
Chopped fresh tarragon, dill or basil

This dish may be prepared in individual baking dishes or one large enough to accommodate servings for 6.

Pour a little of the hot butter into a heatproof baking dish or individual dishes and place the tomato halves in it, cut-side up. Slip an egg on top of each tomato half and cook over low heat for 2 minutes to soften the tomato a little.

Sprinkle eggs with salt and pepper and pour remaining butter over. Sprinkle with chopped herb. Cover lightly with aluminum foil and set aside until ready to cook.

To cook: Bake in a preheated 325° F. (170° C.) for 20 minutes, or until eggs are set to taste. Serve with sautéed chicken livers and hot corn bread.

EGGS PAVAROTTI

---

8 Poached Eggs (page 21)
8 sautéed Round Croutons, about 2½
    inches (6 centimeters) in diame-
    ter (page 149)
½ cup (125 grams) Mushroom
    Duxelles (page 202)

2 cups (½ liter) Mushroom Sauce
    (page 201)
Chopped parsley

Prepare all the ingredients for this dish in advance. Keep the Poached Eggs moist in cool water until ready to assemble and serve.

To serve: Reheat the eggs to just serving temperature in hot water.

Spread croutons with Mushroom *Duxelles*. Drain an egg and place one on each crouton. Pour ¼ cup (60 milliliters) of the Mushroom Sauce over each egg and sprinkle with a little chopped parsley. Serves 4.

You might begin with fresh pineapple and serve croissants with comb honey with the eggs and beverage.

EGGS FLORENTINE

3 cups (¾ liter) Medium Cream
    Sauce (page 199)
2 pounds (1 kilogram) fresh spinach,
    trimmed and cooked
Dash nutmeg to taste

6 Poached Eggs (page 21)
½ cup (60 grams) grated Parmesan
    cheese
½ cup (60 grams) dry bread crumbs
2 tablespoons (30 grams) butter

Prepare Medium Cream Sauce and keep warm.

Cook spinach, drain well and stir in ½ cup (125 milliliters) of the cream sauce. Spread spinach mixture in bottom of six individual baking dishes or a shallow 1-½-quart (1-½-liter) baking dish. Sprinkle with nutmeg.

Stir all but 2 tablespoons (15 grams) of the cheese into remaining cream sauce and cook, stirring, until cheese is melted and sauce is smooth.

Make six depressions in the spinach and slip a poached egg into each. Pour sauce over the spinach. Combine bread crumbs and remaining cheese and sprinkle over sauce. Dot with butter. Cool and refrigerate if necessary.

You can easily make this recipe the day before. To reheat: Bake in a preheated 400° F. (200° C.) oven for 20 minutes if at room temperature; 25 to 30 minutes if refrigerated, or until sauce is bubbling and crumbs are brown.

Serve with bran muffins or buttered whole wheat toast. A fresh fruit compote makes a refreshing start. Serves 6.

Old-Fashioned English Breakfasts

In this age of nutritional knowledge, trimmer figures and fast-paced living, we cannot advocate a return to the bountiful English breakfasts of the 19th century, when a dish of hot cereal with sugar and heavy cream was only the beginning. Since we are increasingly aware of health, and more involved in athletics and exercise, it might not be a bad idea to consider a return to at least a hearty breakfast, enough to fortify our bodies with the energy needed to face any activity that the day might offer. The following rib-sticking egg dishes are patterned on some of the popular breakfast dishes of Victorian England.

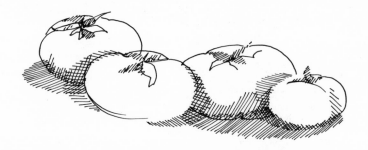

SCRAMBLED EGG PLATTER

4 thinly-sliced pieces of bacon
4 breakfast sausages
1 ripe tomato
Salt and pepper to taste

Butter
Regular Scrambled Eggs for 2 (page 18)

Fry bacon until crisp and golden. Drain well. Sauté breakfast sausages and keep warm. Cut ripe tomato in half, sprinkle with salt and pepper, dot with butter and broil or grill until nicely browned, but not mushy, about 10 minutes.

Scramble eggs and pile in center of a large warm platter. Arrange tomatoes, bacon and sausages around the edge. Serve with hashed brown or pan-fried potatoes and hot muffins or biscuits. Serves 2. A baked apple makes a nice starter.

PLANKED EGGS

2 cups (500 grams) hot mashed pota-
    toes
4 Fried Eggs (page 22)

4 tomato halves, fried or broiled
4 strips crisp Baked Bacon (page 30)

Put potatoes into a pastry bag fitted with a large fluted tube and pipe a heavy ring of potatoes around edge of an oiled hardwood oven plank.

Place Fried Eggs in center of plank with tomatoes on one side and bacon strips on the other.

Place plank under broiler or grill heat for about 2 minutes, or until potato is peaked and brown. Serve immediately. Serves 2.

Try berries and a sliced banana with cream for a first course. Buttered bran muffins go nicely with the planked eggs.

EGGS LYONNAISE

2 tablespoons (30 grams) butter
4 medium onions (2 cups or 250
    grams), sliced ¼-inch (½-centi-
    meter) thick
Coarsely ground black pepper and salt
    to taste

4 eggs
½ cup (125 milliliters) light cream
Chopped parsley

In medium-sized frying pan heat butter. Add onions and sprinkle with salt and pepper. Cover and cook over low heat for about 15 minutes, or until onions are transparent.

Turn onion slices carefully with a pancake turner. Break and slip eggs from a saucer into the onions. Add cream. Cover and continue to cook over medium heat until eggs are cooked to desired firmness.

Sprinkle with parsley and serve immediately. Serves 2. Serve with Grilled English Muffins (page 150), marmalade or strawberry jam. You might serve cranberry or orange juice first, then a bowl of your favorite cereal.

FARMER'S BREAKFAST

6 slices bacon
¾ cup (90 grams) chopped green pepper or capsicum
½ cup (60 grams) chopped onion
6 cups (1½ kilograms) diced, cooked potatoes

Salt and freshly ground pepper to taste
Dried leaf thyme, crumbled, to taste
6 eggs
½ cup (60 grams) shredded Swiss cheese

In a 12-inch (30-centimeter) frying pan cook bacon until crisp and golden brown. Remove from pan and keep warm. Pour off all but 3 tablespoons (45 milliliters) bacon drippings from frying pan. Add green pepper, onion, potatoes, salt, pepper and thyme. Cover and cook for 10 minutes. Remove cover, lift mixture with a pancake turner to thoroughly turn and mix potatoes. Cover and cook for 10 minutes longer. Mix again thoroughly.

Make six identations in potato mixture; break an egg into each indentation. Cover and cook over low heat until eggs are almost set, about 3 minutes. Sprinkle with cheese, crumble bacon on top, cover and continue to cook until cheese is melted and eggs are the desired firmness, about 5 minutes more. Serves 6.

Serve with hot corn bread and honey. For a starter nothing can top a piece of just-ripe melon with a wedge of fresh lime. And, believe it or not, pass the pepper grinder. It adds an unbelievable touch to melon.

EGGS RIALTO

½ pound (250 grams) fresh mushrooms, sliced
6 tablespoons (90 grams) butter
6 eggs
3 tablespoons (45 milliliters) heavy or thick cream
Salt and pepper to taste

1 teaspoon (5 milliliters) Worcestershire sauce
1 teaspoon (2 grams) minced onion
1 tablespoon (8 grams) chopped parsley
2 tablespoons (15 grams) grated Parmesan cheese

Sauté mushrooms in 2 tablespoons (30 grams) of the butter until lightly browned.

In a large frying pan melt remaining butter. Beat eggs lightly with the cream and sprinkle with salt and pepper. Stir in Worcestershire sauce and onion. Scramble eggs in the hot butter until thick and creamy, stirring constantly. Add mushrooms and sprinkle with parsley and cheese. Continue to cook and stir for a few moments longer or until eggs are set but still glossy. Serve on hot buttered toast or in toasted Croustades (page 150). Serves 3.

POACHED EGGS WITH SHERRY SAUCE

1 cup (¼ liter) Medium Cream Sauce
   (page 199)
2 egg yolks, lightly beaten
⅓ cup (40 grams) shredded Gruyère
   or Swiss cheese
Salt and pepper to taste
2 tablespoons (30 milliliters) sherry

4 slices tomato, sautéed in butter
4 slices Canadian or lean bacon,
   sautéed in butter
2 Grilled English Muffins (page 150)
4 Poached Eggs (page 21)
Watercress for garnish

Heat Medium Cream Sauce until bubbling. Remove from heat and stir in egg yolks, cheese and salt and pepper to taste. Stir over low heat for about 3 minutes, or until cheese is melted and sauce is smooth. Do not let sauce boil. Stir in sherry.

Place 1 slice each tomato and bacon on top of each half muffin. Place a Poached Egg on top of the bacon and spoon the sherry sauce over top of eggs. Garnish with watercress. Serves 2. Stewed prunes or figs with cream are nice first, and hot croissants or freshly baked Danish pastry are a good accompaniment.

Hunt Country Breakfasts

This spectacular feast is part of the great tradition of the English-speaking world. It originated in England where sportsmen rode to hounds with the fox as quarry and returned, usually victorious, to an enormous sideboard breakfast.

The popularity of the hunt breakfast spread to the United States in the 18th century, and the sideboard buffet became as much of a tradition as the pink coats of the riders.

For any breakfast buffet table, it is important that you serve only egg dishes that will not lose their palatability if kept waiting for a short time. Here are some suggestions:

SCOTCH EGGS

6 Hard-Boiled Eggs (page 16), well chilled
1 pound (500 grams) breakfast sausage meat
2 tablespoons (15 grams) finely chopped parsley

Coarsely cracked black pepper to taste
½ cup (50 grams) flour
2 eggs, beaten
¾ cup (90 grams) fine bread crumbs
Vegetable oil for frying

Peel eggs and set aside.

Combine sausage, parsley and pepper and divide into six equal portions.

Gently roll each egg in flour to coat, then press meat mixture around eggs with hands, keeping the oval shape.

Dip eggs into beaten egg and roll in bread crumbs.

Heat vegetable oil in deep saucepan to 350° F. (180° C.). Cook one egg at a time for about 4 to 5 minutes or until nicely browned. Drain on paper toweling.

Serves 6, hot or cold. Recipe may be made proportionately larger. Any of the mayonnaise sauces in Chapter 10 is good with the cold eggs; the cheese, mushroom or tomato sauces in the same chapter are excellent with the hot eggs.

EGGS BEAUREGARD

8 Hard-Boiled Eggs (page 16), shelled
6 green peppers or capsicums
4 tablespoons (60 grams) butter
3 tablespoons (18 grams) flour
1 cup (¼ liter) milk

Salt and pepper to taste
½ cup (60 grams) shredded Cheddar cheese
3 slices white bread

Chop eggs coarsely and set aside.

Cut peppers in half, discard seeds and membrane. Place in simmering water for 5 minutes. Drain and place cut side of peppers down on absorbent paper to drain thoroughly.

Make a thick cheese sauce: Melt 3 tablespoons (45 grams) butter in a medium-sized saucepan. Stir in flour and cook until mixture bubbles. Gradually stir in milk and cook, stirring, until sauce is smooth and thick. Add salt, pepper and cheese and continue to stir until cheese is melted. Remove from heat and stir in chopped eggs.

Fill pepper halves with egg mixture and arrange in an oiled shallow baking pan about 12 x 8 inches (30 x 20 centimeters).

Spread bread with remaining butter and cut into ¼-inch (5-millimeter) cubes. Sprinkle bread over filling in peppers.

Bake in a preheated 375° F. (190° C.) oven for about 20 minutes, or until bread cubes are golden and sauce is bubbling.

Serve in the baking dish. Keep hot if necessary over a dish warmer or spirit burner. Serves 6. Recipe may be doubled.

EGGS HUNTER'S STYLE

½ pound (250 grams) chicken livers, cut into small pieces

2 tablespoons (15 grams) finely chopped scallions or spring onions

4 tablespoons (60 grams) butter

6 eggs

Salt and white pepper to taste

Parsley clusters for garnish

Sauté chicken livers and onions in 3 tablespoons (45 grams) butter for 4 to 5 minutes, or until lightly browned.

Spread liver mixture in bottom of a shallow baking dish about 11 x 7 inches (27 x 17 centimeters). Break and slip eggs into the dish, sprinkle with salt and pepper and dot each with a bit of the remaining butter.

Bake in a preheated 325° F. (170° C.) oven for 15 to 20 minutes, or until eggs are set to taste.

Garnish baking dish with parsley and take to table. Keep warm, if necessary, over a dish warmer or spirit burner. Serves 6. Recipe may be doubled. If so, use a 12 x 8-inch (30 x 20-centimeter) shallow baking dish.

EGGS DIABLE

2 cups (½ liter) Light Cream Sauce (page 200)
Salt, pepper and nutmeg to taste
6 tablespoons (90 grams) butter
4 scallions or spring onions, finely chopped
2 teaspoons (10 milliliters) wine vinegar

1 tablespoon (15 grams) prepared mustard
1 tablespoon (2 grams) hot curry powder or to taste
2 egg yolks
6 tablespoons (90 milliliters) heavy or thick cream
8 Hard-Boiled Eggs (page 16), shelled

Season Light Cream Sauce with salt, pepper and nutmeg to taste. Set aside.

In a medium-sized saucepan melt 2 tablespoons (30 grams) of the butter and sauté scallions until golden.

Add vinegar, mustard and curry powder and cook, stirring, for 2 to 3 minutes. Stir in cream sauce and heat to simmering.

Combine egg yolks and cream with a little of the hot sauce before stirring into remaining cream sauce.

Slice and add Hard-Boiled Eggs. Cook over low heat while gradually stirring in remaining 4 tablespoons (60 grams) butter, bit by bit. Do not let sauce boil.

Take to the buffet table in a chafing dish set over hot but not boiling water.

Serve on hot buttered toast, in Individual Tart Shells (page 112) or in toasted Croustades (page 150). Serves 6. Recipe may be doubled.

EGGS À LA MARYLAND

¼ cup (60 grams) butter
1 cup (¼ liter) light cream
½ pound (250 grams) flaked crabmeat
Salt and pepper to taste

12 eggs, lightly beaten
2 tablespoons (15 grams) finely chopped parsley

In a large frying pan melt butter. Add cream, crabmeat, salt and pepper and heat to simmering.

Pour eggs into crabmeat mixture in fry pan and cook over moderate heat, lifting bottom and sides of the mixture as it thickens. As the cooked mixture is lifted, the uncooked part will flow to bottom of the pan. Cook until eggs are thickened but are still moist and creamy, about 6 minutes.

Transfer eggs and crabmeat to a chafing dish or casserole and sprinkle with parsley. Keep warm over hot but not boiling water. Serves 6. Recipe may be doubled.

BUFFET EGGS WESTERN-STYLE

4 slices bacon
1 small onion, chopped
1 small green pepper or capsicum,
    seeded and chopped
1 clove garlic, chopped
8-ounce (250-gram) can tomato sauce

Salt and pepper to taste
Chili powder to taste
8 eggs
½ cup (60 grams) shredded Swiss or
    Monterey Jack cheese

Sauté bacon until crisp, drain on paper towel, crumble and set aside.

Pour off all but 1 tablespoon (15 milliliters) drippings in pan and in it sauté onion, green pepper and garlic over medium heat until vegetables are soft.

Add tomato sauce, salt, pepper and chili powder. Bring to boil, stirring, then lower heat and simmer for 15 minutes.

Spoon the sauce into bottom of a shallow baking dish, about 11 x 7 inches (27 x 17 centimeters) and sprinkle with the crumbled bacon. Break and slip eggs into the sauce and sprinkle eggs with shredded cheese.

Bake in a preheated 350° F. (180° C.) oven for 15 minutes, or until eggs are done as desired.

Take to buffet table in the casserole and keep warm over a dish warmer or spirit burner, if necessary, but try to serve immediately. For an extra touch of the West, serve a spoonful of refried beans on the side. Serves 8. Recipe may be doubled using larger baking dish.

SCOTCH WOODCOCK

2 ounces (56 grams) anchovies in pure
    olive oil
6 slices buttered toast
12 egg yolks

1½ cups (375 milliliters) heavy or
    thick cream
½ cup (125 grams) butter
Freshly ground pepper

Mash anchovy fillets in enough oil from the can to make a smooth paste. Spread on the toast and cut toast into finger lengths. Set aside and keep warm.

Beat egg yolks and gradually beat in the cream. Pour into a double boiler or saucepan placed over simmering water, with butter and pepper to taste. Cook, stirring frequently with a wooden spoon, until egg yolks and cream are like a creamy custard.

Take to table over the hot water; eggs will keep warm until ready to serve. Put anchovy toast in a basket and cover with a napkin. To serve: Ladle the custard over the toast and serve with broiled ripe tomatoes. Serves 6.

3

Economical Luncheon and Supper Dishes

In this chapter, naturally compatible foods—eggs and cheese, eggs and vegetables, eggs and dairy products—team together to bring you irresistible dishes, salads and sandwiches that are nutritious and economical. In fact, eggs are the most economical source of highest-quality complete protein. (Compare the price of a dozen large eggs, which weigh 1½ pounds or 750 grams, with the price per pound of beef, poultry or pork.) Eggs are quick, too, designed to meet the stringent demands of today's cooks. When guests pop in, you can always be the perfect host or hostess with a dozen eggs in the refrigerator.

BAKED EGGS FONDUE

4 eggs, separated
¾ cup (180 milliliters) milk
1 cup (125 grams) shredded Cheddar
    cheese
3 cups or 6 slices (375 grams) fresh
    bread cubes

A dash of dry mustard
Dash of freshly ground pepper
Salt, if needed, to taste

In small mixing bowl beat egg yolks until thick and pale in color, about 5 minutes. Set aside.

In large saucepan combine milk and cheese over moderate heat until cheese is melted. Remove from heat and stir in bread cubes, mustard, pepper and salt. Blend in egg yolks.

In large mixing bowl beat egg whites until stiff but not dry. Fold bread mixture into egg whites. Pour into buttered 1½-quart (1½-liter) baking dish. Set dish in a 2-inch (5-centimeter) deep baking pan set on rack and fill pan with hot water to a depth of 1 inch (2.5 centimeters).

Bake in a preheated 325° F. (170° C.) oven for 55 to 60 minutes, or until a knife inserted near center comes out clean. Serve immediately. Serves 6.

BAKED EGGS AND RICE WITH CHEESE SAUCE

4 tablespoons (60 grams) butter
½ cup (60 grams) finely chopped
    green pepper or capsicum
½ cup (60 grams) sliced fresh mush-
    rooms
3 tablespoons (18 grams) flour
Salt and freshly ground pepper to
    taste

2 cups (½ liter) milk
1 cup (125 grams) shredded American
    or Cheddar cheese .
3 cups (750 grams) cooked rice
6 eggs

Butter a 13 x 9-inch (32 x 22-centimeter) shallow baking dish.

In saucepan melt butter and sauté green pepper and mushrooms for about 5 minutes, or until vegetables are tender, but not brown. Stir in flour, salt and pepper. Gradually stir in milk and cook, stirring constantly, until sauce is thickened and bubbling. Remove from heat, add cheese and stir until cheese is melted.

Combine 1½ cups (375 milliliters) of the cheese sauce with the cooked rice and spread mixture in bottom of prepared dish. Make six indentations with back of a spoon in the rice and carefully break an egg into each indentation.

Bake in preheated 350° F. (180° C.) oven for 20 minutes, or until eggs are set to desired degree. Serve with remaining cheese and mushroom sauce. Serves 6.

GRATINÈE LYONNAISE PÉPIN

2 tablespoons (30 grams) butter
1 very large onion, thinly sliced
3 cups (¾ liter) beef consommé or
 chicken broth
Salt and freshly ground white pepper
 to taste

4 slices firm-textured bread, toasted
¾ cup (90 grams) shredded Gruyère
 or Swiss cheese
3 egg yolks
¾ cup (180 milliliters) port wine or
 Madeira

In a large saucepan melt butter and sauté sliced onion for about 10 minutes, or until a very pale brown. Add broth, salt and pepper, bring to a boil and simmer for 10 minutes.

Meanwhile cut each slice of toast into eight squares. Place one-third of the toast in bottom of a large ovenproof casserole and sprinkle with one-third of the cheese. Add more toast, then more cheese, saving enough to sprinkle over top of the broth. Fill casserole with hot broth, sprinkle with remaining cheese and bake in a preheated 400° F. (200° C.) oven for 25 to 30 minutes.

Take the *gratinée* to the table. Combine yolks and wine in a bowl and whip hard with a fork. With soup ladle make a hole in the gratinée, pour in the egg mixture and combine gently with the soup. Serves 4 to 6.

GOLDEN BUCK

2 eggs
2 cups (250 grams) shredded Cheddar
 cheese
½ cup (125 milliliters) milk
1 tablespoon (15 grams) butter
1 tablespoon (6 grams) flour
2 teaspoons (10 grams) prepared
 mustard

1 teaspoon (5 milliliters) Worcestershire sauce
Salt and pepper to taste
3 Grilled English Muffins (page 150),
 buttered
6 Poached Eggs (page 21)
Watercress or parsley for garnish

In medium-sized saucepan beat eggs. Stir in cheese, milk, butter, flour and seasonings. Cook, stirring constantly, over low heat until cheese melts and mixture is smooth.

To serve: Spoon 2 tablespoons (30 milliliters) sauce over each muffin half. Top each with a Poached Egg and cover each egg with 2 more tablespoons sauce. Garnish with watercress or parsley. Serves 3.

EGGS CREOLE

2 tablespoons (15 grams) chopped
    onion
1 tablespoon (15 grams) butter or
    bacon drippings
½ pound (250 grams) mushrooms,
    sliced
½ cup (60 grams) chopped celery
1 green pepper or capsicum, seeded
    and cubed
1-pound, 4-ounce (564 grams) can
    whole tomatoes, chopped

3 tablespoons (45 grams) tomato paste
Salt and coarsely ground black pepper
    to taste
Dash of cayenne pepper or hot pepper
    flakes
A dash each, thyme and basil
8 Hard-Boiled Eggs (page 16), shelled
    and halved

Cook onion in butter or bacon drippings until tender but not browned. Add mushrooms and sauté for about 2 minutes, stirring constantly.

Add remaining vegetables, tomato paste, salt and pepper. Bring to a boil. Simmer, stirring occasionally, until vegetables are just tender and mixture is medium thick. Add cayenne pepper or hot pepper flakes to taste. Add thyme, basil and eggs. Heat until eggs are just heated through.

Serve with crusty bread to mop up extra sauce or over cooked rice. Serves 4.

TYROLESE DOUBLE-EGG PIE

3 ripe tomatoes, thickly sliced
4 tablespoons (60 grams) butter
2 tablespoons (15 grams) chopped
    parsley
1 tablespoon (8 grams) chopped
    chives
6 tablespoons (48 grams) dry bread
    crumbs

6 Hard-Boiled Eggs (page 16), shelled
    and sliced
6 eggs
Salt and pepper to taste
2 cups (½ liter) light cream

Butter a 9 x 9-inch (22 x 22-centimeter) baking dish. Cover bottom of dish with tomato slices. Dot tomatoes with half the butter and sprinkle with parsley and chives.

Melt remaining 2 tablespoons (30 grams) butter and brown bread crumbs lightly.

Cover tomatoes with alternate layers of egg slices and buttered crumbs. Beat the 6 eggs lightly with salt and pepper. Gradually beat in cream. Pour mixture carefully over ingredients in baking dish and bake in a preheated 375° F. (190° C.) oven for 35 minutes, or until custard is set. Serve with hot baking powder biscuits or bran muffins. Serves 6.

SWISS CHEESE CHARLOTTE

6 slices bread
3 tablespoons (45 grams) butter
6 thin slices lean bacon
¼ pound (125 grams) Swiss cheese, shredded
3 eggs

1½ cups (375 milliliters) milk
½ cup (125 milliliters) heavy or thick cream
Dash of dry mustard
Salt, pepper and nutmeg to taste
Watercress for garnish

Butter a shallow 1½-quart (1½-liter) baking dish. Spread bread slices with butter and cut into ½-inch (1-centimeter) squares. Fry bacon slices until crisp. Drain on absorbent paper.

Starting with bread, make layers of bread and cheese in the prepared dish. Beat eggs with milk, cream and seasonings. Pour egg mixture over bread and let stand for at least 1 hour.

Bake in a 375° F. (190° C.) oven for 30 to 35 minutes, or until well puffed and golden.

Crumble bacon on top, garnish with watercress and serve immediately. Serves 4.

CHEESE STRATA

---

12 slices bread
6 tablespoons (90 grams) butter
½ pound (250 grams) Cheddar
    cheese, shredded
Paprika
6 eggs
2 cups (½ liter) milk

1 cup (¼ liter) light cream
Salt to taste
Dash of cayenne pepper
1 tablespoon (8 grams) chopped
    parsley
1 large ripe tomato (optional)

Butter a 13 x 9-inch (32 x 22-centimeter) shallow baking dish. Spread bread slices thinly with butter.

Line baking dish with half the bread and top with a layer of half the cheese. Repeat bread and cheese layers and sprinkle generously with paprika.

Combine eggs, milk, cream, salt and cayenne. Pour over bread and cheese, being careful that each slice is thoroughly moistened. Refrigerate for at least 3 hours or overnight.

Bake, uncovered, in a 325° F. (170° C.) oven for 35 minutes. Sprinkle with parsley and, if desired, arrange slices of tomato on top. Return to oven and bake for 15 to 20 minutes longer, or until puffy and golden brown. Serves 6.

CURRIED EGG STRATA

¼ cup (60 grams) mayonnaise
1 tablespoon (2 grams) curry powder
4 slices firm whole wheat bread,
    lightly toasted
4 slices firm white bread, lightly
    toasted
4 Hard-Boiled Eggs (page 16), shelled
    and sliced

¼ cup (30 grams) chopped scallions
    or spring onions
½ cup (60 grams) Swiss cheese,
    shredded
3 eggs
2½ cups (625 milliliters) light cream
    or rich milk
Salt and pepper to taste

Combine mayonnaise and curry powder in cup or small bowl. Spread on 2 slices of the whole wheat and 2 slices of the white bread. Cut slices into quarters and arrange in bottom of a buttered 1½-quart (1½-liter) shallow baking dish.

Spread sliced eggs on top and sprinkle with chopped onions and cheese. Cut remaining bread into quarters and arrange in checkerboard style over cheese.

Beat eggs, light cream or milk, salt and pepper. Pour over bread. Cover and refrigerate for at least 1 hour or overnight.

Bake, uncovered, in a preheated 375° F. (190° C.) oven for 45 minutes, or until puffed and golden. Remove to wire rack and let stand for 10 minutes before serving. Serves 4.

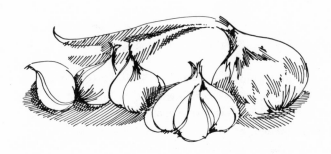

FETTUCCINE WITH EGGS AND ANCHOVIES

4 tablespoons (60 grams) butter
2 tablespoons (30 milliliters) olive oil
   or other vegetable oil
1 clove garlic, minced
2-ounce (60-gram) can anchovy fillets,
   drained
4 tablespoons (30 grams) minced
   parsley
1 teaspoon (2 grams) chopped capers

4 Hard-Boiled Egg yolks (page 16),
   mashed
2 tablespoons (30 milliliters) wine
   vinegar
Generous amount of freshly ground
   black pepper
1 pound (454 grams) fettuccine
Parmesan cheese

In medium-sized saucepan heat butter and oil until it sizzles a drop of water. Add garlic and anchovies and sauté for about 8 minutes, or until mixture has a sauce consistency. Add parsley, capers and egg yolks. Stir in vinegar and pepper. Blend all ingredients thoroughly and simmer for 5 minutes.

Cook fettuccine until just bite-tender, drain and empty into a warm serving bowl. Pour sauce over and toss thoroughly. Serve immediately with grated Parmesan cheese. Serves 4.

EGG AND NOODLE CASSEROLE

6 ounces (180 grams) egg noodles
4 tablespoons (60 grams) butter
½ cup (60 grams) minced onion
½ cup (60 grams) chopped green pepper or capsicum
4 tablespoons (24 grams) flour
1-pound (454-gram) can whole tomatoes

1 cup (125 grams) shredded Swiss cheese
Salt and pepper to taste
8 Hard-Boiled Eggs (page 16), shelled and sliced

Cook noodles according to package directions. Drain, rinse well with cold water and set aside.

In frying pan melt butter and sauté onion and green pepper over moderate heat until tender, but not brown. Stir in flour. Add tomatoes and cook, stirring constantly, until mixture is thickened and bubbling. Add cheese and stir until cheese is melted. Stir in salt and pepper to taste.

Butter a 2-quart (2-liter) casserole. Arrange half the noodles in the casserole. Arrange half the sliced eggs over noodles and cover with half the tomato mixture. Top with remaining noodles and sliced eggs and pour remaining tomato mixture over entire mixture.

Bake in a preheated 350° F. (180° C.) oven for 25 minutes, or until thoroughly heated. Serves 4.

HAM AND EGGS DIDGERIDOO

1½ cups (375 grams) diced boiled ham
2 tablespoons (30 grams) butter
8 eggs
¼ cup (60 milliliters) milk

Salt and freshly ground pepper to taste
2 tablespoons (15 grams) chopped chives or fresh dill

In a medium-sized frying pan brown ham lightly in butter.

Mix remaining ingredients with a fork. Pour over ham and cook over medium heat. As eggs begin to set, gently lift cooked portions so the thin uncooked portion can flow to the bottom of the fry pan. Cook until eggs are thickened throughout but still moist. Serve with sliced ripe tomatoes. Serves 4.

FRENCH OMELET (Basic Recipe)

No other dish is easier to make (once you know how) or is more adaptable to any occasion than a plain, or French, omelet.

It is essential to have an 8- to 10-inch (20- to 25-centimeter) omelet pan with rounded shoulders to help slide the omelet easily onto the plate. It should be well-seasoned or have a nonstick surface. Reserve your omelet pan for omelets only. After making an omelet do *not* wash the pan. Wipe it out with paper towels to preserve the oily surface. If particles of egg adhere, rub it clean with salt and a few drops of oil. Store in a plastic bag.

A perfect omelet is pure gold—never brown—light and delicate in texture, soft and voluptuous in the center, or what the French call *baveuse*. It should take no longer than one minute to make.

3 eggs (at room temperature)
Pinch salt
1 tablespoon (15 milliliters) cold
    water

1 tablespoon (15 grams) unsalted or
    Clarified Butter (page 191)

Break eggs into a bowl, add salt and cold water and beat lightly with a fork until whites and yolks are just blended. Overbeating can result in a tough omelet.

Heat an omelet pan over moderately high heat until a drop of water sizzles and evaporates immediately. Add the butter and as soon as it begins to give off a nutty aroma, but before it browns, give the eggs a few last strokes with the fork and pour them into the pan.

With the left hand, shake the pan continuously back and forth over the heat and, at the same time, stir eggs briskly with the flat side of the fork held in the right hand to heat all the liquid evenly. (It's a little like rubbing your tummy and patting your head at the same time!)

When eggs are thickened but are still soft and moist, stop stirring but continue to shake the pan and, with the fork, quickly smooth the egg evenly in the pan.

If the omelet is to be filled, now is the time to sprinkle the filling over the moist surface of the eggs, fold the omelet and turn it out onto a warm serving plate. To do this: Grasp handle of the pan in the left hand, thumb and fingers uppermost. Trade your fork for a rubber scraper, tip pan at a 45° angle and push the egg at the upper one-third of pan toward the center, shaping eggs into a plump half-moon. Quickly run the scraper around the edge of omelet and under the far side to make sure it is not stuck to the pan.

Still holding pan at a 45° angle, place lip of the pan slightly off-center of the serving plate. Whack the handle of the pan to encourage the omelet to turn over onto itself, then tip it out onto the plate. Spread with a little soft butter and serve immediately. Serves 1.

Once you have learned to make a plain omelet you can make variations ad infinitum by the addition of herbs, vegetables, meats or seafood and by garnishing it with commercial sour cream or a savory sauce. The following are some ideas:

Cheese Omelet

Add 3 tablespoons (25 grams) shredded Gruyère or grated Parmesan cheese to the beaten eggs. Use very little salt, if any.

Herb Omelet

Add 1 teaspoon (2 grams) each minced parsley, chives and tarragon to the beaten eggs.

Tomato Omelet

Peel, seed and dice a ripe tomato. Cook tomato in a little butter until it is reduced to a thick moist puree. Season with salt and pepper and use to fill an omelet.

Omelette Paysanne

Add some diced sautéed bacon, chopped scallions or spring onions and parsley to eggs before cooking.

Mushroom Cream Omelet

Cook a few sliced fresh mushrooms in a little heavy or thick cream until tender, then proceed according to basic recipe and fold in mushroom-cream mixture.

Omelette Lyonnaise

Mince 1 small onion and sauté gently in butter until tender. Add 1 tablespoon (8 grams) minced parsley to the 3 beaten eggs, pour over onion and proceed according to the basic recipe.

Curried Chicken Liver Omelet

Sauté 3 tablespoons (45 grams) chopped chicken livers with a dash of curry powder in 1 tablespoon (15 grams) butter for 5 minutes, or until chicken livers are done. Sprinkle with salt and pepper. Make an omelet according to basic recipe. Fill with half of the chicken liver mixture, roll and turn out on warm serving plate. Make a slit in center and spoon remaining chicken liver filling in the slit.

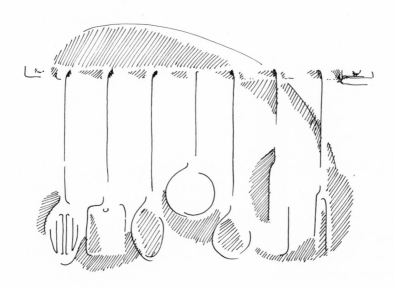

PRINCESS OMELET

4 eggs
¼ cup (60 grams) commercial sour
    cream
2 teaspoons (4 grams) minced onion
Dash of crushed red pepper

Salt to taste
3-ounce (90-gram) package cream
    cheese, cut into bite-sized cubes
1 tablespoon (15 grams) butter

Combine eggs, sour cream, onion, red pepper and salt. Fold in cream cheese.

In omelet pan heat butter until it sizzles a drop of water. Pour egg mixture into the hot butter. As the mixture thickens at the edges, draw these portions toward center with a fork so the uncooked portions flow to bottom. Shake pan back and forth over heat to keep omelet from sticking. When eggs are set but still moist, fold omelet with help of a rubber scraper and empty out onto a warm serving dish. Serve immediately. Serves 2. Delicious served with fresh asparagus or new garden peas.

SPANISH OMELET

1 medium onion, minced
1 green pepper or capsicum, seeded
   and chopped
1 clove garlic, minced
2 tablespoons (30 milliliters) olive oil
2 fresh tomatoes, peeled, seeded and
   chopped or 1-pound can (454
   grams) whole tomatoes, drained
   and chopped

Salt to taste
Dash of cayenne pepper
6 eggs

Cook onion, green pepper and garlic in olive oil for 10 minutes, or until vegetables are soft but not brown. Add tomatoes, salt and cayenne and simmer for 20 minutes, or until most of the excess liquid has cooked away but mixture is still soft and moist.

Make two 3-egg omelets, one at a time, according to the basic recipe (page 61). Fill each with a spoonful of the savory mixture, fold and turn out onto warm serving plates. Pour any remaining sauce around them. Serves 2.

EGG FOO YUNG (A Chinese-style Omelet)

6 eggs
1 cup (250 grams) fresh or canned
   bean sprouts, rinsed and drained
1 small onion, chopped
3 to 4 mushrooms, chopped
½ to 1 cup (125 to 250 grams)
   chopped cooked chicken

2 teaspoons (10 milliliters) soy sauce
Salt to taste
Vegetable oil
Egg Foo Yung Sauce (recipe follows)

In a large bowl beat eggs until foamy. Stir in bean sprouts, onion, mushrooms, chicken, soy sauce and salt.

Heat a small frying pan, about 6 inches (15 centimeters) in diameter. Add 1 tablespoon (15 milliliters) oil and heat until it sizzles a drop of water. Pour one-quarter of the egg mixture (about ½ cup or 125 milliliters) into fry pan and cook for 1 to 2 minutes, or until crisp and golden on underside; turn with a wide pancake turner and cook for 1 minute longer. Fold in half and arrange on warm serving plate. Keep warm while making 3 more omelets with remaining egg mixture. Serves 4.

Serve each omelet with Egg Foo Yung Sauce.

Egg Foo Yung Sauce

Mix 1 tablespoon (15 grams) cornstarch or cornflour and 1 tablespoon (15 milliliters) soy sauce in a small saucepan. Gradually stir in 1 cup (¼ liter) chicken broth. Cook, stirring, until sauce simmers and thickens. Makes 1 cup (¼ liter).

SOUFFLÉ OR PUFFY OMELET (Basic Recipe)

In the soufflé or puffy omelet the eggs are separated, the yolks beaten until light in color and the whites until stiff. Often an extra white for every two yolks is used and the beaten whites are folded lightly into the yolks and seasonings. When cooked, it will puff to double its depth and should be rushed to the table. Any vegetable puree or savory sauce may be used as a garnish.

4 to 6 egg whites	Freshly ground white pepper
4 egg yolks	2 tablespoons (30 milliliters) water
Dash salt	2 tablespoons (30 grams) butter

Beat egg whites until stiff but not dry in a large bowl.

Beat egg yolks with salt and pepper in a small bowl until thick and lemon colored. Beat in water.

Fold half the egg whites into the yolk mixture lightly but thoroughly. Add remaining egg whites and fold in lightly.

In a 9-inch (22.5-centimeter) frying or omelet pan with an ovenproof handle (or wrap handle in aluminum foil) heat the butter. Swirl pan to coat bottom and sides. Pour in egg mixture and cook over low heat for 5 minutes, or until eggs are set and golden brown on bottom. Transfer to a preheated

375° F. (190° C.) oven and bake for 10 minutes, or until puffy and lightly tinged with brown on top.

Loosen omelet around edge of pan with a knife; lift omelet onto a heated serving plate. Cut a gash with a knife down center of omelet and fold in half with a wide spatula. Turn out onto warm serving plate. Serve immediately. Serves 2.

PUFFY SPANISH OMELET

6 eggs, separated
3 tablespoons (45 milliliters) water
Salt and freshly ground black pepper
    to taste
4 tablespoons (60 grams) butter
1 medium onion, sliced
1 small green pepper or capsicum,
    seeded and diced

Dash each of dried oregano, cayenne
    and salt
3 medium tomatoes, peeled, seeded
    and coarsely chopped
1 cup (250 grams) commercial sour
    cream
2 tablespoons (15 grams) chopped
    chives

Using above ingredients, make and bake a Puffy Omelet (page 65) according to basic recipe but use only half the amount of butter.

While omelet is baking, sauté onion and green pepper in remaining 2 tablespoons (30 grams) butter in frying pan for about 5 minutes, or until vegetables are soft.

Add oregano, cayenne, salt to taste and tomatoes and cook just until tomatoes are heated through.

Remove omelet from oven. Loosen around edge with a knife; cut a gash down the center, spread tomato mixture over one side of omelet, fold and turn onto warm serving plate. Top omelet with sour cream and sprinkle with chives. Serve immediately. Serves 4.

Puffy Omelet with Cheese Sauce

Make a Swiss Cheese Sauce (page 201). Set aside.

Make and bake a Puffy Omelet following basic recipe (page 65).

After you have cooked and transferred it to a warm serving plate, cut a gash down the center with a knife and spoon ¾ cup (180 milliliters) of the Swiss Cheese Sauce over the omelet. Fold in half with a wide spatula and spoon remaining sauce over top. Serves 2.

Puffy Mushroom Omelet
Cook ¼ pound (125 grams) fresh sliced mushrooms in 2 tablespoons butter (30 grams) for about 5 minutes. Make a Puffy Omelet according to basic recipe (page 65). When puffed and golden, transfer to a warm platter, score down center and spoon mushroom mixture over it. Fold in half and serve immediately. If desired, serve with either Mushroom, Light Cream or Swiss Cheese Sauce (pages 201, 200 and 201). Serves 2.

FRITTATA

For the timid soul who fears to try his hand at a French Omelet, an Italian *frittata* may be the answer. Traditionally it is cooked until the bottom is set but top is still runny and then flipped over in mid-air to cook on the other side. Setting it under a hot broiler or grill for a few minutes gives better results, and there is no danger of the *frittata's* landing on the floor! Neither top nor bottom should be brown. A *frittata* is traditionally cut into wedges and served directly from the frying pan or it may be loosened with a spatula and slipped onto a warm platter before it is cut.

1 tablespoon (8 grams) chopped scallions or spring onions	9 eggs
3 tablespoons (45 grams) butter	3 tablespoons (45 milliliters) heavy or thick cream
1 cup (125 grams) chopped fresh mushrooms	Salt and pepper to taste
½ cup (125 grams) chopped ham	3 tablespoons (25 grams) freshly grated Parmesan cheese

Sauté onions in 1 tablespoon (15 grams) of the butter until transparent. Add mushrooms and ham and continue to cook until mushrooms are tender.

Beat eggs lightly with cream and salt and pepper. Pour over vegetable-ham mixture in frying pan and cook over low heat for 20 minutes, or until eggs are almost set but still runny on top. Sprinkle with cheese and place under broiler or grill heat for 2 to 3 minutes, or until eggs on top are set. Cut into pie-shaped wedges to serve. Serves 6.

ZUCCHINI OR COURGETTE FRITTATA

3 tablespoons (45 grams) butter
1 small onion, chopped
2 small zucchini or courgette, sliced
Dash of oregano
10 eggs
½ cup (125 milliliters) heavy or thick
    cream

Salt and freshly ground pepper to
    taste
1 large ripe tomato, peeled and thinly
    sliced

In an ovenproof 10-inch (25-centimeter) omelet pan or frying pan, heat butter. Add onion, zucchini and oregano and sauté over moderate heat, stirring often, until zucchini is partially cooked.

Combine eggs, cream, salt and pepper until blended. Pour into pan over zucchini, cover and cook over low heat for 20 minutes or until eggs are partially set.

Arrange tomato slices in a single layer on top of *frittata* and transfer to a preheated 350° F. (180° C.) oven. Bake for 10 minutes, or until eggs are set and tomatoes are cooked. Loosen *frittata* around side of pan with spatula. Cut into wedges to serve. Serves 6.

SCHOOL-DAY EGG BURGERS

¾ pound (375 grams) pork sausage
    meat
2 tablespoons (30 milliliters) sausage
    drippings
2 tablespoons (15 grams) finely
    chopped green pepper or
    capsicum

2 tablespoons (15 grams) finely
    chopped onion
6 eggs, lightly beaten
Salt and pepper to taste
4 hamburger or sandwich buns, split
    and buttered

Form sausage meat into 4 patties and sauté in a frying pan over moderate heat until cooked through.

While sausage is cooking, remove 2 tablespoons drippings (30 milliliters) and pour into an 8-inch (20-centimeter) frying pan. In it sauté green pepper and onion until onion is tender but not browned.

Combine eggs and seasonings. Pour into frying pan over green pepper and onion, and scramble eggs and vegetables until eggs are cooked throughout, but are still moist and glossy.

To serve: Place a sausage patty on each top half of bun. Place bottom half of bun beside the sausage and spoon scrambled eggs on top. Serves 4.

HAM 'N' CHEESE SANDWICH PUFF

2 slices day-old bread
Butter
1 slice Swiss or Cheddar cheese
1 slice ham

2 eggs
½ cup (125 milliliters) milk
A little freshly ground pepper
Dash of dry mustard

Trim crusts from bread and butter each slice on one side only. Place a slice, buttered side down, in a shallow baking dish or pan, about 5 x 5 x 1½ inches (12 x 12 x 3 centimeters). Top with slice of cheese and top cheese with ham slice. Cover with remaining bread slice, buttered side up.

Beat together eggs, milk and seasonings. Pour evenly over sandwich. Bake in preheated 350° F. (180° C.) oven for 35 to 40 minutes, or until knife inserted near center of sandwich comes out clean. Serves 1.

Note: Recipe may be doubled. For two sandwiches use a small loaf pan, 8 x 4 inches (20 x 10 centimeters) or any shallow pan that will accommodate the sandwiches in a single layer. Bake as above.

EGG AND HERB SANDWICHES

4 Hard-Boiled Eggs (page 16), shelled
    and chopped
4 tablespoons (60 grams) mayonnaise
    or commercial sour cream
Salt to taste

Dash of paprika
1 tablespoon (8 grams) chopped
    chives
Dash of dried or chopped fresh dill
4 slices whole wheat bread, buttered

Combine eggs with mayonnaise or sour cream, salt, paprika, chives and dill. Spread thickly between two slices bread, and cut into halves or quarters. Serves 2.

The following are quick and simple variations of egg fillings. Combine all ingredients and season to taste with salt and pepper. Chill until ready to spread between buttered slices of rye, whole wheat or pumpernickel bread. Each filling makes enough for 2 sandwiches.

Zesty Cheese and Egg Sandwich Filling

½ cup (125 grams) cream-style cottage cheese
2 Hard-Boiled Eggs (page 16), shelled
and chopped
2 tablespoons (15 grams) chopped dill
pickle

1 tablespoon (8 grams) chopped
radish
1 teaspoon (2 grams) minced onion
2 tablespoons (30 grams) mayonnaise

Chicken and Egg Sandwich Filling

1 cup (250 grams) ground or minced
cooked chicken
2 Hard-Boiled Eggs (page 16), shelled
and chopped

1 teaspoon (2 grams) grated onion
with juice
1 tablespoon (8 grams) minced parsley
3 tablespoons (45 grams) mayonnaise

Sardine and Egg Sandwich Filling

1 cup (250 grams) mashed sardines
2 Hard-Boiled Eggs (page 16), shelled
and chopped
1 teaspoon (5 milliliters) lemon juice

2 tablespoons (15 grams) chopped
pimento
1 teaspoon (2 grams) minced onion
⅓ cup (75 grams) mayonnaise

EGG AND POTATO SALAD

1 pound (454 grams) small new
potatoes
Salt and freshly ground black pepper
to taste
2 tablespoons (30 milliliters) wine
vinegar

5 tablespoons (75 milliliters) salad oil
1 tablespoon (8 grams) chopped
chives
1 anchovy fillet, minced
4 Hard-Boiled Eggs (page 16), shelled

Boil potatoes in their skins until tender. Drain and peel when cool enough to handle.

In salad bowl combine salt, pepper, vinegar and salad oil. Stir in chives and anchovy fillet.

Remove yolks from egg whites, add to salad dressing and mash and mix well.

Slice egg whites into slivers and add to dressing. Slice in potatoes. Mix lightly and serve cold. Serves 4.

SALADE NIÇOISE

Mixed salad greens, washed and dried
2 6½-ounce (195-gram) cans solid
    white tuna fish
2 ounces (60 grams) anchovy fillets in
    olive oil
4 ripe tomatoes, quartered
4 Hard-Boiled Eggs (page 16), shelled
    and quartered

1 green pepper or capsicum, seeded
    and cut into strips
Ripe olives
1 tablespoon (8 grams) capers
Pimento, cut into strips for garnish
Vinaigrette Sauce (page 208)

Arrange salad greens in center of a large platter.

Drain oil or liquid from tuna fish and arrange tuna in center of salad greens. Surround by anchovy fillets, tomatoes, eggs, green pepper and ripe olives.

Sprinkle with capers and garnish with pimento strips. Just before serving pour 1 cup (250 milliliters) Vinaigrette Sauce over all and serve with additional dressing on the side. Serves 4.

SPINACH EGG SALAD WITH SWEET AND SOUR DRESSING

1 pound (454 grams) fresh spinach
½ cup (125 milliliters) salad oil
¼ cup (60 grams) sugar
1 teaspoon (2 grams) grated onion
2 tablespoons (30 milliliters) vinegar
Dash each of salt and dry mustard
6 slices Baked Bacon, cooked until
    crisp, drained and crumbled
    (page 30)

5 Hard-Boiled Eggs (page 16), shelled
    and chopped
1 Hard-Boiled Egg (page 16), shelled
    and sliced

Wash spinach thoroughly and discard thick stems. Drain and chill to crisp.

Combine oil, sugar, onion, vinegar, salt and mustard. Beat or blend until thick and syrupy and sugar is completely dissolved.

Tear spinach into bite-sized pieces in a large salad bowl. Add bacon and chopped eggs. Pour dressing over all and let stand about 30 minutes. Toss salad to mix well. Garnish with egg slices. Serves 6. Both the greens and the dressing in this recipe may be prepared well ahead of time and refrigerated until you are ready to mix them.

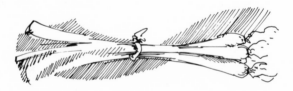

EGG SALAD LOUIS

Mixed salad greens
9 Hard-Boiled Eggs (page 16), shelled
    and quartered
2 ripe tomatoes, cut into wedges

1 avocado, peeled and sliced length-
    wise
Louis Dressing (page 208)

Wash salad greens and drain well. Cut or tear greens into bite-sized pieces and pile into a large salad bowl. In center of bowl arrange eggs on top of the greens. Around the eggs alternate wedges of tomato and avocado slices. Serve with Louis Dressing. Serves 4.

MOLDED EGG SALAD

---

12 Hard-Boiled Eggs (page 16),
   shelled
2 envelopes (15 grams) unflavored
   gelatin
½ cup (125 milliliters) water
1 cup (250 milliliters) chicken broth
1½ cups (375 grams) Mayonnaise
   (page 207)
2 tablespoons (30 milliliters) lemon
   juice

1 teaspoon (2 grams) salt
3 drops Tabasco or another hot pepper sauce
1½ cups (185 grams) finely chopped
   parsley
½ cup (60 grams) finely chopped
   green pepper or capsicum
2 tablespoons (15 grams) minced scallions or spring onions

Cut 6 eggs in lengthwise slices, reserving center slice of each egg for garnish. Separate remaining eggs. Force yolks through a fine sieve and set aside. Chop whites finely and reserve.

Soften gelatin in cold water. Heat chicken broth to boiling, add gelatin and stir until thoroughly dissolved. Pour one-third cup (75 milliliters) of the gelatin mixture into bottom of a 1½-quart (1½-liter) ring mold. Arrange center slices of the eggs in a circle around bottom. Chill until set.

Combine egg yolks, Mayonnaise, lemon juice, half the salt, the hot pepper sauce and half the remaining gelatin. Spoon mixture over egg slices, sprinkle with parsley and green pepper and chill until set.

Combine remaining gelatin with egg whites, onions and remaining salt. Spoon into mold and chill for 6 to 8 hours. Unmold on large platter and garnish as desired. Serves 8 to 10.

4
Brunch
and Other
Elegant Egg Dishes

There is such a wealth of brunch and other elegant egg dishes for entertaining that it is hard to know where to begin. I shall start with a few of my favorites, followed by some delicate quiches and their cousins, timbales; then move on to sublime savory mousses, glamorous crepes and sky-high soufflés.

EGGS BENEDICT

4 Grilled English Muffins (page 150)
16 thin slices Canadian or lean bacon
8 Poached Eggs (page 21)

Hollandaise Sauce (page 205)
Parsley or watercress to garnish

Broil or grill muffins until nicely browned. Keep warm.
Sauté the bacon until edges are lightly browned. Set aside.
Poach the eggs and keep moist in warm water.
Make Hollandaise Sauce.
Serve 2 eggs per person: Top each English muffin half with 2 slices bacon, then with a poached egg. Spoon Hollandaise Sauce over each egg and garnish with parsley spray or sprig of watercress. Serves 4.

EGGS SARDOU

14-ounce (420-gram) can artichoke
    bottoms
1 pound (454 grams) fresh spinach,
    trimmed, cooked and well
    drained

½ cup (125 milliliters) Medium
    Cream Sauce (page 199)
Dash nutmeg
8 Poached Eggs (page 21)
Hollandaise Sauce (page 205)

Drain and rinse artichoke bottoms. Cover with boiling water and set aside.

Puree the spinach in a blender container, food processor or food mill and mix with Medium Cream Sauce and nutmeg. Heat to serving temperature in a small saucepan.

Poach eggs and make Hollandaise.

Place two artichoke bottoms per serving on a warm plate, hollow side up. Fill hollows with creamed spinach and top each with a poached egg. Coat each egg with Hollandaise Sauce. Serves 4.

POACHED EGGS EN COCOTTE WITH SHRIMP OR PRAWNS

½ cup (125 grams) cooked minced
    shrimp or prawns
1 tablespoon (15 grams) soft butter
1 egg yolk
½ cup (60 grams) soft white bread
    crumbs
¼ cup (60 milliliters) heavy or thick
    cream

1 tablespoon (8 grams) minced parlsey
Salt and freshly ground white pepper
    to taste
4 eggs
2 teaspoons (10 grams) butter

Mix the shrimp or prawns to a paste, the tablespoon soft butter, egg yolk, bread crumbs, cream, parsley, salt and pepper.

Line bottom and sides of four buttered cocottes, ramekins or custard cups with the mixture. Slip an egg into each dish and top each egg with ½ teaspoon (2½ grams) butter.

Set dishes into a saucepan of simmering water to reach almost to top of the dishes. Cover and cook over low heat for 6 to 10 minutes, or until eggs are set to desired degree.

Serves 4. Lobster or crabmeat may be substituted for the shrimp.

QUICHE LORRAINE (Basic Recipe)

Quiche selections begin with the original classic quiche as made in the French province of Lorraine. It also happens to be my favorite quiche.

Pastry for a One-Crust Pie (page 159)
½ pound (250 grams) lean bacon slices
½ pound (250 grams) Gruyère cheese, diced

6 egg yolks
1½ cups (275 milliliters) heavy or thick cream
Dash each, salt, mustard and freshly ground black pepper

Roll out pastry and line a 9-inch (22.5-centimeter) pie dish or fluted quiche dish. Trim overhang to ½ inch (1 centimeter), turn under flush with rim and flute to make a stand-up edge. Prick shell evenly all over with a fork and partially bake in a preheated 425° F. (220° C.) oven for 6 minutes; remove to wire rack to cool.

Fry bacon in a medium-sized fry pan until crisp. Drain on absorbent paper.

Crumble bacon onto bottom of partially baked pie shell and cover with diced cheese.

Beat egg yolks lightly. Slowly beat in cream, salt, mustard and pepper.

Place pie dish on a rimmed baking sheet; pour in egg mixture. Bake in a preheated 350° F. (180° C.) oven for about 40 minutes or until center is almost set, but is still soft. Do not overbake; custard will continue to cook as it cools. Let stand 5 to 15 minutes before cutting and serving. Serves 6.

MUSHROOM QUICHE

Pastry for a One-Crust Pie (page 159)
½ pound (250 grams) fresh mushrooms, sliced
½ cup (60 grams) sliced scallions or spring onions
1 tablespoon (15 grams) butter
¼ pound (125 grams) Swiss cheese, shredded

4 eggs, beaten
1 cup (¼ liter) light cream
¼ cup (30 grams) grated Parmesan cheese
Salt and freshly ground pepper to taste

Follow basic recipe for Quiche Lorraine (page 77), partially baking a 9-inch (22.5-centimeter) pie shell.

In large frying pan over moderate heat cook mushrooms and onions in butter until mushrooms are lightly browned, 6 to 8 minutes. Spread mushroom mixture into bottom of pie shell and sprinkle with Swiss cheese.

Combine eggs with remaining ingredients. Pour over mushroom mixture. Bake in a preheated 375° F. (190° C.) oven for 35 to 40 minutes, or until knife inserted near center comes out clean. Let stand 10 minutes before serving. Serves 6.

QUICHE AMÉRICAINE (Basic Recipe for Leftovers)

You can use this basic recipe for any kind of leftover. Cooked flaked fish, ground beef or cooked chopped vegetables can replace the chicken. Vary the herb to suit your particular taste. Use milk in place of light cream if you are watching calories.

Pastry for a One-Crust Pie (page 159)
¼ pound (125 grams) Swiss cheese, shredded
½ cup (125 grams) finely chopped cooked chicken meat
6 eggs, beaten

1½ cups (375 milliliters) light cream
Salt and freshly ground pepper to taste
Dash of dried tarragon or other favorite herb

Make and partially bake a One-Crust 9-inch (22.5-centimeter) pie shell according to basic Quiche Lorraine recipe (page 77).

Sprinkle cheese and chicken into pie shell. Combine eggs and remaining ingredients. Pour over cheese-chicken mixture. Place shell on rimmed baking sheet and bake in a preheated 350° F. (180° C.) oven for 35 to 40 minutes, or until knife inserted near center comes out clean. Let stand for 10 minutes before serving. Serves 6.

CRAB QUICHE

Pastry for a One-Crust Pie (page 159)
6 ounces (180 grams) shredded, cooked crabmeat or lobster
½ cup (60 grams) shredded Swiss cheese
1½ cups (375 milliliters) light cream
6 eggs, beaten

1 tablespoon (8 grams) minced scallions or spring onions
½ teaspoon (1 gram) salt
Dash of dry mustard
Dash of crumbled dried tarragon or ½ tablespoon (4 grams) chopped fresh tarragon

Follow basic recipe for Quiche Lorraine (page 77), partially baking a 9-inch (22.5-centimeter) pie shell.

Sprinkle crabmeat or lobster and cheese on bottom of pastry shell. Place pie dish on a baking sheet.

Combine remaining ingredients and pour over crabmeat and cheese.

Bake in a preheated 375° F. (190° C.) oven for 30 to 35 minutes, or until a knife inserted near center comes out clean. Let stand for 10 minutes before serving. Serves 6.

TOMATO BROCCOLI QUICHE

Pastry for a One-Crust Pie (page 159)
4 cups (750 grams) chopped fresh broccoli
1 medium onion (½ cup or 60 grams), chopped
2 tablespoons (30 grams) butter
2 tablespoons (30 milliliters) water
1 cup (¼ liter) light cream
2 eggs

½ cup (60 grams) shredded Swiss cheese
Salt and pepper to taste
Dash of ground nutmeg
1 cup (125 grams) freshly grated Parmesan cheese
½ cup (60 grams) dry bread crumbs
3 medium tomatoes, thinly sliced

Roll pastry out into a 15 x 11-inch (37 x 27-centimeter) rectangular and fit into an 11 x 7-inch (27 x 17-centimeter) baking dish. Turn edges under and press to sides.

In large frying pan over moderate heat cook broccoli and onion, covered, with butter and water until just tender, about 5 minutes. Remove from heat.

In medium-sized bowl beat together cream and eggs; stir in Swiss cheese, salt, pepper and nutmeg. Add broccoli mixture.

Combine Parmesan and bread crumbs. Sprinkle ⅓ cup (40 grams) bread mixture on bottom of pie crust. Dip tomato slices on both sides in bread mixture and arrange half in a layer in the shell. Pour broccoli mixture over tomatoes. Arrange remaining tomatoes, overlapping, along the long edges of the dish. Sprinkle any remaining cheese mixture on top.

Bake in a preheated 375° F. (190° C.) oven for 60 minutes, or until top is puffy and a knife inserted near center comes out clean. Cool 15 minutes before cutting and serving. Serves 8.

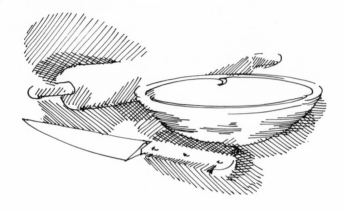

ALPINE CHEESE TARTS

Pastry for two crusts (page 159)
1 medium-sized onion, chopped (½ cup or 60 grams)
2 tablespoons (30 grams) butter
4 eggs, separated
1½ cups (375 milliliters) commercial sour cream
Salt and pepper to taste

2 tablespoons (15 grams) grated Parmesan cheese
½ pound (250 grams) Swiss cheese, cut into ½-inch (1-centimeter) cubes
1 tablespoon (8 grams) chopped parsley

To make tart shells: Roll out pastry, half at a time, ⅛-inch (3-millimeters) thick, on tea towel or lightly floured pastry cloth; cut three 6-inch (15-centimeter) rounds from each half (a saucer makes a good pattern). Fit each round into a 4-inch (10-centimeter) tart-shell tin, pressing pastry firmly against bottom and sides. Trim overhang to ½ inch (1 centimeter), turn under flush with rim and flute to make a stand-up edge. Prick shells all over with a fork and bake in a preheated 450° F. (230° C.) oven for 5 minutes. Remove from oven and lower oven temperature to 325° F. (170° C.).

Meanwhile sauté onion in butter until soft; spoon into partially baked shells, dividing it equally.

Beat egg yolks lightly in a medium-sized bowl. Stir in sour cream, salt, pepper and Parmesan. Set aside 18 Swiss cheese cubes, then fold remainder into egg mixture. Spoon over onion in the tart shells.

Bake tarts in the 325° F. (170° C.) oven for 15 minutes.

While tarts bake, beat egg whites until they form soft peaks in another medium-sized bowl. Remove tarts from oven; spoon beaten egg whites over each, swirling them in attractive patterns with back of the spoon. Top each tart with three of the cheese cubes.

Bake for another 10 minutes, or until meringue is golden and cheese is melted. Sprinkle with parsley and serve immediately. Serves 6.

TIMBALES (Basic Recipe)

Timbales are similar to quiches but are not framed with a flaky crust.

1 cup (250 grams) of any cooked chopped vegetables, meat or fish*	½ teaspoon (1 gram) salt Dash of paprika 1 cup (¼ liter) hot milk
½ cup (60 grams) shredded Swiss or Cheddar cheese	1 tablespoon (8 grams) grated Parmesan cheese
4 eggs	Mornay Sauce (page 200)
1 tablespoon (8 grams) minced onion	

In bottom of four 6- to 9-ounce (180- to 270-gram) buttered custard cups or ramekins, sprinkle ¼ cup (60 grams) chopped vegetables, meat or fish and 2 tablespoons (15 grams) Swiss or Cheddar cheese.

Combine eggs, onion, salt and paprika. Gradually beat in hot milk. Pour into prepared cups, dividing equally, and sprinkle with Parmesan cheese.

Set cups in a shallow baking pan and pour hot water into pan to within ½ inch (1 centimeter) of top of custard mixture.

* Suggestions include: broccoli, cauliflower, spinach, sautéed chopped mushrooms, turkey, chicken, ham, shrimp, prawns, crabmeat, tuna or salmon.

Bake in preheated 350° F. (180° C.) oven for 25 to 30 minutes, or until knife inserted near center comes out clean.

Remove cups from hot water. Gently loosen edges with knife or spatula and invert onto serving plates. Serve with Mornay Sauce. Serves 4.

CHICKEN LIVER TIMBALES

2 tablespoons (30 grams) butter
2 tablespoons (12 grams) flour
1 cup (¼ liter) hot milk
½ teaspoon (1 gram) salt
Dash white pepper
½ pound (250 grams) chicken livers
2 eggs

2 egg yolks
6 tablespoons (90 milliliters) heavy or thick cream
2 tablespoons (30 milliliters) port, Madeira or. Cognac
Béarnaise Sauce (page 206)

Butter eight small ramekins, each about 4-ounce (125-gram) capacity.

In saucepan melt butter and stir in flour. Cook, stirring, until mixture bubbles. Remove from heat and add hot milk, all at once. Stir vigorously until blended. Add salt and pepper, return to moderate heat and cook, stirring constantly, until mixture is smooth and thick. Cool, stirring occasionally.

Put livers, eggs and egg yolks into container of an electric blender and blend at high speed for 1 minute.

Combine sauce, cream, wine or Cognac and the liver mixture and strain through a fine sieve. Pour into prepared ramekins, filling each almost to the top.

Set ramekins in a shallow pan containing 1 inch (2.5 centimeters) hot water. Bake in a preheated 350° F. (180° C.) oven for 30 minutes, or until knife inserted in center comes out clean. Turn out onto individual serving plates and serve with Béarnaise Sauce. Serves 8.

MOUSSE DE FOIE GRAS

Savory mousses are delicate egg dishes and are always cooked or chilled in a mold, depending on whether they are to be served hot or cold. They are usually served sauced.

1 cup (250 grams) cooked pureed white meat of chicken
1 cup (250 grams) puree of foie gras
¼ cup (60 milliliters) heavy or thick cream

4 tablespoons (60 milliliters) Madeira wine
Salt and pepper to taste
3 egg whites
Madeira Sauce (page 202)

Combine chicken, foie gras, cream, Madeira wine, salt and pepper.

Beat egg whites until stiff but not dry and fold into chicken mixture. Turn into a buttered 4-cup (1-liter) mold. Set mold in a shallow pan containing 1 inch (2.5 centimeters) hot water and bake in a preheated 350° F. (180° C.) oven for 30 minutes.

Run a knife around edge of mold and invert mousse on a warm serving dish. Serve with Madeira Sauce. Serves 4.

SPINACH MOUSSE

2 cups (1 pound or 454 grams) cooked pureed spinach
3 eggs, lightly beaten
¼ cup (60 milliliters) heavy or thick cream

¼ cup (60 grams) butter, melted
1½ cups (185 grams) bread crumbs
Dash of pepper
1 teaspoon (2 grams) salt
Easy Creamed Eggs (page 35)

Brush a 1-quart (1-liter) ring mold with butter.

Combine spinach, eggs, cream, butter, bread crumbs, pepper and salt. Spoon into prepared mold. Set mold in shallow pan containing about 1 inch

(2.5 centimeters) of hot water and bake in a preheated 350° F. (180° C.) oven for 40 minutes, or until set.

Remove mold from oven and run a knife around edges. Unmold on serving platter and fill center with Creamed Eggs. Serves 4.

COLD CHICKEN MOUSSE

1 envelope (8 grams) unflavored gelatin
1 cup (¼ liter) chicken broth
3 egg yolks
Salt to taste
Pinch white pepper
1 cup (250 grams) cooked ground or minced chicken meat

1 cup (¼ liter) heavy or thick cream, whipped
½ cup (125 milliliters) Mayonnaise (page 207)
Lettuce, radish roses and watercress for garnish

Soften gelatin in half the broth. Beat egg yolks and stir in remaining broth, salt and pepper. Pour mixture into a saucepan and cook over simmering water, stirring constantly, until thickened to custard consistency. Stir in softened gelatin and remove from heat.

Add chicken and stir mixture over a bowl of cracked ice until mousse begins to set.

Fold in whipped cream and Mayonnaise.

Turn mixture into a 1-quart (1-liter) mold rinsed with cold water. Chill for several hours until set. Turn out on serving platter and garnish with lettuce, radish roses and watercress. Serves 4.

FILLETS OF SOLE JOINVILLE

One of the most elegant luncheon dishes in the world is Fillets of Sole Joinville. I would not recommend that any cook attempt the recipe or its basic fish mousse or accompanying sauce without a blender or food processor. The mousse and sauce may be made a day in advance and kept refrigerated.

9 fillets of lemon sole or flounder
¾ pound (375 grams) raw turbot, pike, sole, flounder or salmon or a combination of two-thirds white fish and one-third shrimp, prawns or salmon
2 egg whites (reserve yolks for the sauce)
White pepper

1 teaspoon salt
1½ cups (375 milliliters) heavy or thick cream
1 tablespoon (15 grams) soft butter for mold
Shrimp or Prawn Sauce (recipe follows)
1 tablespoon (8 grams) chopped parsley

Cut fillets in half lengthwise and remove any tiny strip of bone that may run down the median line. Wash and dry well.

Butter a 1½-quart (1½-liter) ring mold and line as follows: Place each fillet in mold, pale side down with narrow ends toward center and broader ends hanging over outer edge. Overlap slightly, fanning them out from center. Refrigerate while making the mousse.

Dice fish and blend or process with egg whites, pepper, salt and cream until smooth.

Fill lined mold with the mousse; fold ends over filling, narrow ends first, then broad outer ends on top. Cover with waxed paper and refrigerate.

About 45 minutes from serving time, discard waxed paper and cover with buttered foil. Set the mold in a pan containing 1 inch (2.5 centimeters) hot water and bake in a preheated 350° F. (180° C.) oven for 30 minutes. Remove, let stand for 5 minutes, then turn out onto serving platter. Mop up any excess liquid that runs onto the platter.

Spoon part of the Shrimp or Prawn Sauce over the mold and serve the rest separately. Sprinkle with parsley before serving. Serves 6.

SHRIMP OR PRAWN SAUCE

½ pound (250 grams) fresh shrimp or prawns
4 tablespoons (60 grams) butter
½ pound (250 grams) mushroom caps, sliced
4 tablespoons (24 grams) flour
1 cup (¼ liter) reduced Fish Stock (page 88) or ½ cup (125 milliliters) each chicken broth and clam juice

2 tablespoons (30 milliliters) sherry
1 tablespoon (15 milliliters) Cognac
Salt and white pepper to taste
½ cup (125 milliliters) heavy or thick cream
2 or 3 egg yolks (reserved from the mousse)
Juice of ½ lemon

Shell and devein shrimp. Put them in a small saucepan and barely cover with water. Bring water to a simmer, remove from heat and let shrimp cool in the liquid. When cool enough to handle, dice shrimp and set aside.

In medium-sized saucepan melt butter and sauté mushrooms for 5 minutes or until wilted. Stir in flour. Remove from heat, add hot Fish Stock all at once, return to heat and cook, stirring or whisking constantly, until sauce is thick and smooth. Stir in sherry, Cognac, salt and pepper to taste. Cook, stirring, for 3 minutes. At this point sauce may be cooled and reheated.

To finish sauce: Heat sauce until very hot. Stir in cream beaten lightly with egg yolks and a little of the hot sauce. Stir in lemon juice and shrimp. Makes about 1 quart (1 liter) sauce.

QUENELLES DE POISSON

The most fanciful among hot mousse dishes are the quenelles or fragile soufflé dumplings floating in a cream sauce. This dish of sheer ambrosia was originally made in Lyons, France, from fresh-water pike. However, any strictly fresh raw white fish such as flounder, sole or turbot may be used. I usually throw in one large or two medium-sized raw, shelled and deveined shrimp or prawns. Ask your fish dealer to give you the head and bones of the fish if you wish to make Fish Stock for the sauce, or you may use bottled clam juice instead.

2 eggs

½ cup (50 grams) flour

Dash of nutmeg

½ teaspoon (1 gram) salt

Freshly ground white pepper or
   cayenne to taste

3 tablespoons (45 milliliters) melted
   butter

½ cup (125 milliliters) hot milk

1 pound (454 grams) boneless fillets
   of fresh pike or other white fish

1 cup (¼ liter) heavy or thick cream,
   very cold

Fish Velouté Sauce (recipe follows)

Freshly grated Parmesan cheese

Separate eggs; reserve whites and drop yolks into a small, heavy saucepan. Add flour, half the nutmeg, salt, pepper or cayenne and all the melted butter. Stir with small wooden spoon to blend. Do not use a whisk.

Gradually stir in hot milk. Blend rapidly over moderately high heat, stirring all around bottom and sides of pan, until mixture pulls away from sides and forms a waxy ball in center. This is called a panade. Refrigerate or put in freezer until very cold, but not frozen.

The fish, too, should be very cold. Cut it into thin strips. Put into a blender or food processor one-half the fish at a time with part of the remaining nutmeg, salt and pepper, one ice cube, half the reserved egg whites (or one) and half the cream. Repeat with second half of ingredients. As each portion is pureed, transfer to an electric mixer. Add the panade and beat vigorously for 3 minutes, or until mixture is creamy and smooth. If not completely smooth, rub it through a food mill.

Up to this point the quenelle mixture may be made a day ahead of time and refrigerated.

To poach: Butter a large aluminum roasting pan about 17 x 12 x 2½ inches (42 x 30 x 6 centimeters). Using two large dessert spoons dipped in water, shape mixture into rounded oval shapes and arrange them neatly in the buttered pan, keeping them at least 1 inch (2.5 centimeters) apart. Butter a length of waxed paper and place it, butter-side down, on top of the quenelles. Gently pour 4 cups (1 liter) boiling water on top of the waxed paper, letting it flow outward into pan. Bring water to a simmer and simmer for 10 to 15 minutes. The paper will prevent the quenelles from forming an unattractive skin.

When poached, transfer quenelles with a slotted spoon to a large, shallow, buttered au gratin dish. Cover with buttered waxed paper and refrigerate up to one day if necessary. May also be frozen for a week or two.

To serve: Cover quenelles generously with Fish Velouté Sauce, spooning sauce over them rather than pouring it. Sprinkle with grated Parmesan and brown under broiler or grill heat for 3 to 4 minutes, or until sauce is bubbling and tinged with brown. Serves 8 (two quenelles each).

FISH VELOUTÉ SAUCE

4 tablespoons (60 grams) butter
4 tablespoons (24 grams) flour
Dash of salt and cayenne
1 cup (¼ liter) Fish Stock (recipe follows) or clam juice
1 cup (¼ liter) heavy or thick cream

¼ cup (30 grams) grated Parmesan or shredded Swiss cheese
2 egg yolks
2 tablespoons (30 milliliters) sherry or Cognac

In saucepan melt half the butter. Stir in flour, salt and cayenne and cook, stirring, until mixture bubbles. Gradually stir in Fish Stock or clam juice and cream and cook, stirring, until sauce is smooth and thickened. Add remaining butter, bit by bit, and the cheese and cook over low heat for 5 minutes.

Set aside at this point, if necessary, and reheat to finish.

To finish sauce: In a cup or small bowl beat egg yolks and sherry or Cognac with a little of the hot sauce. Stir into remaining sauce and heat without boiling. Makes about 3 cups. Mushroom Sauce (page 201) may be substituted for the fish sauce. My preference is the Velouté.

To make Fish Stock: Place fish head and bones in medium-sized saucepan, cover with 3 cups (¾ liter) cold water, add 1 diced carrot, a few sprigs of parsley, 1 minced scallion or green onion and salt and pepper to taste. Simmer for 20 minutes. Makes 2 cups (½ liter).

CHEESE SOUFFLÉ (Basic Recipe)

The secret of a soufflé is in the proper beating of the eggs and the incorporation of the beaten whites into the basic mixture. Separate eggs carefully. The tiniest speck of yolk in the whites will keep them from beating to their lightest. Allow egg whites to sit at room temperature before beating and, when possible, add one or two extra egg whites. The best proportion is four whites to every three yolks. Beat yolks and stir into the sauce while sauce is still hot; the heat of the sauce partially cooks the yolks. Let the mixture cool a little before adding the whites.

The egg whites must be mixed into the yolk mixture as gently as possible to retain as much of the air beaten into them as possible. The best tool for doing this is a large metal spoon which cuts cleanly down through the mixture. First, stir in a couple of large spoonfuls of the beaten whites (about one-fourth of the total amount) to thin down the yolk mixture. Stir this amount in until no speck of white may be seen. Then cut in remaining egg whites. Fold down from top of mixture to bottom of bowl, then up against side of bowl. Rotate the bowl frequently and continue until all whites have been mixed in and there are no large streaks of either white or yellow.

Bake the soufflé on a rack in the center of the oven for the time given in recipe, then test: Shake the dish gently; if center is firm, it should be done. Use a pot holder to protect your hand and give the dish a little shake. If it shimmies all over, it is not done. If it shimmies just a little in the center, it is still creamy in center and should cook for 5 minutes longer if you wish the soufflé completely set. Always serve a soufflé immediately.

Once prepared, bake a soufflé as soon as possible, but if necessary, you may hold the soufflé for as long as one hour before baking it if you cover the dish and mixture with a large saucepan or kettle to keep drafts away.

3 tablespoons (45 grams) butter	Dash of dry mustard
2 tablespoons (12 grams) flour	Dash salt
1 cup (¼ liter) hot milk	Coarsely ground black pepper
2 teaspoons (10 grams) cornstarch (or cornflour)	4 egg yolks
	1 tablespoon (8 grams) grated Parmesan cheese
1 tablespoon (15 milliliters) water	
1 cup (125 grams) shredded Cheddar or Swiss cheese	6 egg whites

In saucepan melt butter. Stir in flour and cook, stirring, until mixture is bubbly. Remove saucepan from heat; add hot milk and beat vigorously until mixture is blended. Return to moderate heat and cook, stirring, for 1 minute. Mix cornstarch with the water and stir into the sauce. Add cheese and cook, stirring, until cheese is melted.

Remove from heat and beat in mustard, salt and pepper.

Beat in egg yolks one at a time and set aside to cool a little.

Prepare a 1–½-quart (1–½-liter) soufflé dish. Butter bottom and sides and sprinkle with grated Parmesan.

Beat egg whites until stiff but not dry. Stir in one-fourth of the egg whites to lighten egg yolk mixture. Fold in remaining egg whites.

Spoon into prepared soufflé dish and set dish into center of a preheated 400° F. (200° C.) oven; immediately turn oven down to 375° F. (190° C.) and bake for 30 minutes, or until done to taste. Serve with any desired sauce. Serves 4.

Here are some variations to try:

Ham Soufflé

Follow basic recipe, substituting 1 cup (250 grams) minced cooked ham for the shredded cheese.

Chicken Soufflé

Follow basic recipe, substituting 1 cup (250 grams) minced cooked chicken for the shredded cheese. A dash of curry powder cooked with the butter-flavor mixture is nice in the sauce. You may also use fine dry bread crumbs in place of the Parmesan cheese.

Vegetable Soufflé

Follow basic recipe, substituting 1 cup (250 grams) cooked, pureed vegetable such as spinach, broccoli, asparagus, corn or carrots for the shredded cheese. Add a dash of nutmeg to the sauce with any green vegetable.

Shrimp, Prawn, Lobster or Crab Soufflé

Follow basic recipe, substituting 1 cup (250 grams) cooked minced lobster, shrimp, prawns or flaked crabmeat for the shredded cheese. Season the sauce to taste with lemon juice and add 1 tablespoon (8 grams) minced parsley to the sauce.

Salmon or Tuna Soufflé

Follow basic recipe, substituting 1 cup (250 grams) cooked, flaked salmon or tuna for the shredded cheese. Add 1 teaspoon (5 milliliters) Worcestershire sauce to the sauce.

QUEEN'S SOUFFLÉ

---

3 tablespoons (45 grams) butter	½ cup (125 grams) cream-style cottage cheese
3 tablespoons (18 grams) flour	
½ teaspoon (1 gram) salt	1 tablespoon (8 grams) chopped parsley
1 cup (¼ liter) milk	
Few drops Tabasco or another hot pepper sauce	1 tablespoon (8 grams) chopped chives
4 ounces (125 grams) cream cheese, softened	6 eggs, separated
	2 additional egg whites if available

In medium-sized saucepan melt butter. Stir in flour and salt and cook, stirring constantly, until mixture bubbles. Stir in milk and Tabasco and continue cooking and stirring until sauce thickens and boils for about 1 minute.

Beat in cream cheese and cottage cheese. Add parsley and chives and beat in egg yolks, one at a time.

Beat egg whites just until soft peaks form. Stir one-fourth of the egg whites into the yolk mixture to thin it a little, then fold in remaining egg whites until no large streaks of white or yellow remain.

Spoon mixture into an ungreased 2-quart (2-liter) soufflé dish. To make a top hat effect, run a rubber spatula in a deep circle in the mixture about 1 inch (2.5 centimeters) from edge.

Bake in a preheated 375° F. (190° C.) oven for 35 minutes, or until puffy, golden and set to taste. Serves 6.

CHEESE ON MUSHROOM SOUFFLÉ

The following is my favorite soufflé. The soufflé mixture is piled on top of a mushroom sauce and then baked.

½ cup (125 grams) butter
¼ cup (30 grams) chopped scallions
or spring onions
1 clove garlic, minced
Dash of curry powder
½ pound (250 grams) fresh mushrooms, sliced
2 tablespoons (30 milliliters) Cognac
or brandy
½ cup (125 milliliters) dry white wine
Salt and pepper to taste
2 teaspoons (4 grams) chopped fresh
tarragon (optional)
4 tablespoons (24 grams) flour

1 cup (¼ liter) thick or light cream
1 tablespoon (8 grams) chopped
parsley
4 tablespoons (30 grams) grated Parmesan cheese
Dash each of cayenne, dry mustard
and salt
1 cup (¼ liter) milk
1 tablespoon (15 grams) cornstarch or
cornflour
3 tablespoons (45 milliliters) water
1 cup (125 grams) shredded Swiss or
Gruyère cheese
6 eggs, separated

In medium-sized saucepan melt half the butter. Add scallions, garlic and curry powder and cook, stirring, over moderate heat for 2 minutes. Add mushrooms and sauté for 2 to 3 minutes longer. Add Cognac, white wine, salt, pepper and tarragon and cook until liquid is reduced to half its original quantity.

Combine 1 tablespoon (6 grams) flour and the cream, stir into mushroom mixture and cook, stirring, until sauce is thickened. Add parsley.

Butter a 2-quart (2-liter) soufflé dish and sprinkle with half the Parmesan cheese. Pour mushrooms and sauce into prepared dish and set aside.

In medium-sized saucepan melt remaining butter. Stir in remaining flour, cayenne, mustard and salt. Gradually stir in milk and cook, stirring, until sauce is smooth and thick. Combine cornstarch and water, stir into sauce and cook, stirring, for 3 minutes longer. Add shredded cheese and remaining Parmesan and stir until cheese is melted. Remove sauce from heat and beat in egg yolks, one at a time.

In large mixing bowl beat egg whites just until soft peaks form. Fold one-fourth of the whites into yolk mixture to lighten it, then fold remaining whites into yolk mixture until no large streaks of yellow or white remain. Spoon gently into soufflé dish over mushrooms and sauce.

Set soufflé on rack in middle of a preheated 400° F. (200° C.) oven. Immediately reduce temperature to 375° F. (190° C.) and bake for 35 to 45 minutes, or until set in center to desired degree. Serve immediately to 4 for lunch; 6 as a first-course appetizer.

Variation: Pile the soufflé mixture on top of either of the following: Lobster-Sherry Sauce or Curried Shrimps or Prawns.

LOBSTER-SHERRY SAUCE

2 tablespoons (30 grams) butter
2 tablespoons (12 grams) flour
1 cup (¼ liter) thick or light cream, according to taste
Salt and cayenne pepper to taste

½ cup (125 milliliters) sherry or Madeira
2 cups (454 grams) freshly cooked lobster meat or meat from 2 small lobsters

In heavy saucepan melt butter. Stir in flour and cook, stirring, until mixture bubbles. Gradually stir in cream and cook, stirring, until sauce is smooth and thick. Season to taste with salt and cayenne. Stir in sherry and simmer for

2 minutes. Remove sauce from heat and add lobster. Pour Lobster-Sherry Sauce into prepared soufflé dish, pile soufflé mixture on top and bake according to basic recipe. Makes about 4 cups (1 liter).

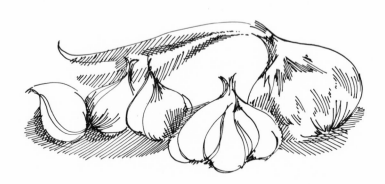

CURRIED SHRIMPS OR PRAWNS

1 pound (454 grams) medium-sized shrimps or prawns, about 24 to 30

3 tablespoons (45 grams) butter

¼ cup (30 grams) finely chopped onion

6 tablespoons (45 grams) finely chopped peeled apple

1 small clove garlic, minced

2 tablespoons (4 grams) curry powder

½ cup (125 milliliters) chicken broth

¼ cup (60 milliliters) tomato sauce

⅔ cup (150 milliliters) heavy or thick cream

Salt to taste

1 tablespoon (6 grams) flour

Shell and devein shrimp or prawns. Rinse under cold water and pat dry.

In a heavy saucepan melt 1 tablespoon (15 grams) butter. In it cook onion, apple and garlic over moderate heat for about 4 minutes, stirring. Add curry powder and cook, stirring, for 1 minute longer.

Gradually blend in chicken broth and tomato sauce and simmer for 2 minutes, stirring. Add cream and salt to taste and simmer about 2 minutes longer.

Combine another tablespoon butter with the flour and add to sauce, bit by bit. Remove sauce from heat.

In a medium-sized frying pan melt remaining tablespoon butter and add the shrimp. Cook over high heat, stirring and shaking the pan for about 3 minutes. Add shrimp to sauce and blend well. Bring sauce and shrimp just to a simmer and pour into prepared soufflé dish. Pour soufflé mixture on top and bake according to basic recipe. Makes 4 cups (1 liter).

BASIC SPONGE ROLL

When a soufflé is cooked on a baking sheet, and rolled around a creamy filling, it is known as a roulade or a sponge roll.

6 eggs, separated

½ teaspoon (1 gram) salt

2 teaspoons (10 milliliters) lemon juice

2 tablespoons (30 milliliters) water

½ cup (50 grams) flour

¼ cup (60 grams) melted butter

Favorite filling (see suggestions that follow)

Oil a 15 x 10 x 1-inch (37 x 25 x 2.5-centimeter) jelly-roll pan or Swiss-roll tin. Line bottom with waxed paper and oil the paper. Set aside.

In large mixing bowl beat egg whites with salt until stiff but not dry, just until whites no longer slip when bowl is tilted.

In another large mixing bowl beat egg yolks until thick and pale in color, about 5 minutes. Gradually beat in lemon juice and water. Sprinkle flour over yolks. Gently fold in beaten whites until thoroughly blended. Pour into prepared pan, spreading batter evenly and well into corners.

Bake in preheated 350° F. (180° C.) oven for 15 minutes, or until sponge layer springs back when lightly touched with fingertip.

Loosen sponge roll from sides of pan with spatula and invert onto a clean kitchen or tea towel. Carefully pull waxed paper off bottom of sponge layer and discard. Cover with fresh sheet of waxed paper. Roll from long side, jelly-roll fashion, rolling waxed paper with it. Wrap in the towel and place seam-side down on wire rack to cool for about 30 minutes.

Meanwhile, make filling and any sauce you might wish to serve with it such as cheese, cream or mushroom.

Unroll sponge layer and brush surface with melted butter. Spread with filling and reroll. Wrap in foil, sealing tightly.

Note: The roll may be made ahead and refrigerated for one or two days or frozen for several weeks before serving.

To Serve: Bake roll in foil wrapping in preheated 350° F. (180° C.) oven for 20 minutes for refrigerated roll; 35 to 40 minutes for frozen.

Slice ½-inch (1-centimeter) thick and serve plain or with a sauce. Makes 12 slices; serves 6. Some filling suggestions. . . .

Ham and Egg Sponge-Roll Filling

1 cup (250 grams) finely chopped
   cooked ham
2 Hard-Boiled Eggs (page 16), shelled
   and chopped
2 tablespoons (15 grams) chopped
   parsley

1 tablespoon (8 grams) minced onion
1 tablespoon (15 grams) prepared
   mustard
2 tablespoons (30 grams) mayonnaise

Combine all ingredients and set aside until needed.

Egg and Chicken Sponge-Roll Filling

6 Hard-Boiled Eggs (page 16), shelled
   and chopped
½ cup (125 grams) chopped cooked
   chicken
½ cup (125 grams) Mayonnaise (page
   207)

¼ cup (30 grams) chopped scallions
   or spring onions with tops
½ teaspoon (1 gram) salt or to taste
Dash of curry powder to taste

In saucepan combine all ingredients and heat to simmering, stirring constantly. Set aside until needed.

BROCCOLI ROULADE

6 tablespoons (90 grams) butter
¾ cup (75 grams) flour
½ teaspoon (1 gram) salt
3½ cups (875 milliliters) milk
1½ cups (185 grams) shredded Swiss
   cheese

6 eggs, separated
1 pound (454 grams) fresh broccoli
Dash of dry mustard

Oil a 15 x 10 x 1-inch (37 x 25 x 2.5-centimeter) jelly-roll pan or Swiss-roll tin; line with foil and oil the foil.

In medium-sized saucepan melt butter. Stir in flour and salt and cook until mixture bubbles. Slowly stir in 3 cups (750 milliliters) milk and cook, stirring, until sauce is smooth and thickened. Remove sauce from heat and pour 1 cup (250 milliliters) into a small saucepan and reserve.

Add ½ cup (60 grams) of the cheese to the larger amount of sauce and stir until cheese is melted.

In small bowl beat egg whites with electric mixer to soft peaks. In a large bowl, and with same beater, beat egg yolks for about 3 minutes, or until thick and pale in color. Beat a small amount of the hot sauce into the egg yolks, then gradually stir in remainder until well-blended.

Beat one-third of the egg whites into the egg-yolk sauce, then fold in remaining egg whites until no streaks of white or yellow remain. Spread mixture evenly in prepared pan.

Bake in a preheated 325° F. (170° C.) oven for 45 minutes, or until top is golden and springs back when lightly touched.

Meanwhile, cut broccoli flowerettes into 2-inch (5-centimeter) lengths, then cut into ½-inch (1-centimeter) pieces. (Save stems for soup.) Cook broccoli pieces in boiling salted water until just tender, about 12 minutes. Drain.

To the reserved sauce add mustard, ½ cup (60 grams) of the cheese and the remaining ½ cup (125 milliliters) milk. Stir over low heat until cheese is melted.

Remove roulade from oven, loosen edges with a spatula and invert onto a strip of aluminum foil. Discard waxed paper from bottom of roulade layer.

Scatter broccoli evenly over surface of roulade, sprinkle with remaining ½ cup cheese and drizzle with ½ cup (125 milliliters) of the sauce.

Starting at narrow 10-inch (25-centimeter) side, roll soufflé, jelly-roll fashion, lifting foil to guide it. Lift roll onto heated platter with two wide spatulas and spoon some of the sauce over the top. To serve: Cut roll into thick slices and serve with remaining sauce. Serves 6 to 8.

C R E P E S (Basic Recipe)

Crepes can be made in quantity and frozen for future use. To freeze, simply stack between layers of waxed paper, put in a sealed container and place in freezer. To use within a day or so, wrap stacked crepes in foil or plastic and refrigerate until about 1 hour before serving.

3 eggs
1 cup (¼ liter) milk
3 tablespoons (45 grams) butter,
    melted

¾ cup (75 grams) flour
½ teaspoon (1 gram) salt

Combine all ingredients in blender container or bowl and blend or beat with a rotary beater or whisk until smooth, about 30 seconds. Pour batter into a pint (½ liter) measuring cup or jug and refrigerate for 1 hour.

Heat an 8-inch (20-centimeter) omelet pan or a 6-inch (15-centimeter) crepe pan over medium-high heat until it sizzles a drop of water.

Brush the pan lightly with soft butter. For each crepe pour in just enough batter to coat bottom of pan with a thin layer. As you pour with jug or cup in right hand, immediately rotate and tilt pan with left hand to swirl the batter quickly and evenly. Then tilt pan over container of batter so that any excess batter will run out. If the crepe has holes, add a drop or two of batter to patch.

Brown crepe on one side. This should take only a minute or so. When evenly browned and set, turn it carefully, using spatula. It's very delicate. Let the other side dry for about one-half minute. It will not be as beautifully browned as the first side, but who cares? This side will be on the inside of the finished crepe.

Invert pan over a strip of paper toweling, emptying out crepe to cool, and repeat until all batter has been used. If your pan does not have a nonstick surface or is not well-seasoned, you may have to brush it with soft butter after each two or three crepes.

As the crepes cool, stack them in a pie dish. Cover with foil or plastic wrap to keep them moist until ready to use.

Makes 16 6-inch (15-centimeter) crepes or 12 8-inch (20-centimeter) crepes.

Note: For dessert crepes, add 2 tablespoons (30 grams) sugar.

CRÊPES AUX FRUITS DE MER

12 crepes (using preceding basic
    recipe)
8 tablespoons (125 grams) butter
½ cup (125 grams) flaked crabmeat
About ¾ cup (180 grams) diced
    cooked lobster (meat of 1 small
    lobster)
½ teaspoon (1 gram) salt
Freshly ground white pepper
1 tablespoon (15 milliliters) dry sherry
4 fresh mushrooms, thinly sliced
Dash of lemon juice

¼ cup (25 grams) flour
Dash cayenne
1 cup (¼ liter) Fish Stock (page 88)
    or clam juice
½ cup (125 milliliters) heavy or thick
    cream
2 egg yolks
2 tablespoons (30 milliliters) sherry
2 tablespoons (15 grams) grated Par-
    mesan cheese
1 tablespoon (15 grams) melted butter

Make crepes and keep moist until needed.

In frying pan heat 2 tablespoons (30 grams) butter. Add crabmeat, lobster, salt and a few grindings of white pepper. Shake pan over moderate heat for 1 to 2 minutes. Add sherry and set aside.

In medium-sized saucepan melt 4 tablespoons (60 grams) butter and sauté mushrooms for 1 to 2 minutes, stirring constantly.

Add lemon juice, pepper and more salt, if desired, to taste and cook over brisk heat for 2 minutes.

Stir in flour and cayenne. Gradually stir in Fish Stock or clam juice and stir over moderate heat until sauce boils.

Stir in remaining butter, bit by bit, and half the cream and simmer for 5 minutes.

Combine egg yolks, sherry and remaining cream with a little of the hot sauce. Stir into remaining sauce and heat without boiling. Stir in half the Parmesan.

Put 1 tablespoon (15 grams) of the crab-lobster mixture on each crepe, roll up and arrange in a buttered au gratin dish. Spoon the sauce over. Sprinkle with remaining Parmesan and the melted butter and brown under broiler or grill heat until sauce is bubbling around edges and is tinged with brown. Serves 6.

CRÊPES VERSAILLES

24 crepes (using Basic Recipe page 96)
¼ pound (125 grams) butter
¾ cup (75 grams) flour
1½ cups (375 milliliters) rich chicken stock
2 cups (½ liter) light cream
½ cup (125 milliliters) white wine
Salt and white pepper to taste
2 pounds (1 kilogram) cooked, finely diced chicken

2 tablespoons (15 grams) each minced chives, parsley and tarragon
1 cup (¼ liter) Mornay Sauce (page 200)
1 cup (¼ liter) Hollandaise Sauce (page 205)
1 cup (¼ liter) heavy or thick cream, whipped

Make crepes and set aside.

In large saucepan melt butter. Add flour and cook, stirring, until mixture bubbles. Gradually stir in chicken stock, light cream and white wine. Season to taste with salt and pepper. Combine with the chicken and herbs.

Put a large spoonful of the chicken mixture on each crepe, roll into a cylinder and arrange in shallow baking dishes.

Combine Mornay and Hollandaise sauces and fold in whipped cream. Spoon over the crepes in a wide ribbon and put under broiler or grill heat until sauce is bubbling and tinged with brown. Serves 12 for lunch or 24 for first-course appetizer.

5
Party Food
and First Courses

Eggs, more than any other single item of food, come to the aid of hosts and hostesses by contributing an impressive list of dishes suitable for any type of casual or formal occasion. In this chapter are canapés, dainty finger sandwiches, deviled eggs, dips, and more fanciful egg dishes that serve as first-course appetizers. These are only a sampling. Throughout the book, many of the lunch and brunch dishes, such as the quiches, soufflés and crepes, may be converted into elegant first-course appetizers simply by making them in miniature or serving them in small portions.

Party Food

PARTY EGG ROLLS

Roll a slice of bread with a rolling pin to flatten. Spread with finely chopped Hard-Boiled Egg (page 16) mixed with mayonnaise seasoned with salt and pepper. Roll up bread slice, cut in half and insert a sprig of watercress into each end of the tiny rolls.

FROSTED PARTY SPECIAL

6 Hard-Boiled Eggs (page 16), shelled
and chopped

4-ounce (125-gram) jar pimentos,
drained and chopped

½ teaspoon (1 gram) salt

6 tablespoons (90 grams) mayonnaise

½ pound (250 grams) boiled ham,
ground or minced

3 medium-sized sweet pickles,
chopped

48 thin slices sandwich bread

8 ounces (250 grams) cream cheese

3 tablespoons (45 grams) commercial
sour cream

3 Hard-Boiled Egg yolks (page 16),
sieved

Parsley for garnish

Combine eggs, pimentos, salt and half the mayonnaise and mix well.

Combine ham, pickles, and remaining mayonnaise and mix.

Cut bread into rounds. Spread 16 slices with egg mixture and top each with a second round, spread with ham mixture and top with third round. Press firmly together.

Mix cheese and sour cream and beat until fluffy. Spread over top and around sides of sandwiches and chill 2 to 3 hours. Before serving, sprinkle sandwiches with sieved egg yolk and garnish with a sprig of parsley. Makes 16 sandwiches.

EGG AND CAVIAR CANAPÉS

Top a buttered, round cut-out of bread with a slice of Hard-Boiled Egg (page 16) and surround by a ring of red caviar. Pile a little chopped purple Spanish onion in center and top this with a dab of commercial sour cream.

TOMATO EGG CANAPÉS

Place a thin slice of small ripe tomato on a round of bread the same size as the tomato slice, spread with mayonnaise. Top tomato with a slice of Hard-Boiled Egg (page 16) and with a pastry bag fitted with a small fluted tube, make a small rosette of mayonnaise in center. Tuck a sprig of parsley into side of mayonnaise rosette.

CHICKEN LIVER CANAPÉS

Pile chopped, cooked chicken livers in center of a round cut-out of bread spread with chicken fat or butter. Make a border around livers with sieved Hard-Boiled Eggs (page 16). Garnish chicken livers with minced onion and parsley and sprinkle with lemon juice.

EGG BUTTER CANAPÉS

Brioche Egg Bread (page 147)   Egg Butter Filling (recipe follows)

For elegant party or wedding canapés, use homemade brioche bread sliced from ¼ to ⅓ inch (5 to 8 millimeters) thick and cut into rounds, squares or rectangles. Spread with Egg Butter Filling.

EGG BUTTER FILLING

Mash ¼ pound (125 grams) butter with two sieved Hard-Boiled Egg yolks (page 16), a dash of white pepper and salt and 1 teaspoon (5 milliliters) lemon juice until smooth and creamy.

EGG AND CUCUMBER BRIOCHE CANAPÉS

Spread top and sides of Brioche Egg Bread (page 147) rounds with mayonnaise. Dip sides in finely chopped parsley to coat. Top with a slice of Hard-

Boiled Egg (page 16) and top the egg with a thin slice of cucumber. Press out a small rosette of mayonnaise in center of cucumber through a pastry bag fitted with a small fluted tube.

EGG AND SARDINE CANAPÉ

Put a small sardine on a rectangular cut-out of bread spread with Egg Butter Filling (page 103) and surround by a border of mayonnaise or Egg Butter pressed out through a pastry bag fitted with a small fluted tube. Sprinkle sardine with a few drops lemon juice, top with overlapping slices of Hard-Boiled Egg (page 16) and sprinkle egg with finely chopped parsley.

CHEESE PUFFS

1 cup (¼ liter) water
¼ cup (60 grams) butter
1 cup (100 grams) flour
Salt to taste
4 eggs

1 cup (125 grams) shredded Cheddar
  cheese
Crabmeat (recipe follows) or other favorite sandwich filling

In a medium-sized saucepan bring water and butter to a rapid boil, stirring until butter melts. Remove from heat. Add flour all at once and stir briskly until paste comes away from sides of pan and forms a smooth ball in center. Add salt and cook over moderate heat for 30 seconds, stirring rapidly.

Remove from heat and stir in eggs, one at a time, beating vigorously after each addition until paste becomes smooth and glossy. Beat in cheese. Drop one-half tablespoon of paste into mounds 2 inches (5 centimeters) apart on baking sheet and bake in a preheated 425° F. (220° C.) oven for 15 minutes; reduce temperature to 350° F. (180° C.) and bake for 10 to 15 minutes longer.

Cool puffs on wire racks. Cut off tops and fill with crabmeat or other favorite filling. Replace tops and keep cold until ready to serve. Makes 32 to 36 hors d'oeuvres.

CRABMEAT FILLING

6 Hard-Boiled Eggs (page 16), shelled and finely chopped

1 cup (250 grams) crabmeat, finely chopped

1 cup (125 grams) chopped celery

½ cup (125 grams) Mayonnaise (page 207)

½ teaspoon (1 gram) salt or to taste

Dash of dry mustard

Mix all ingredients thoroughly. Fill cheese puffs, or you can spread filling on cocktail crackers for canapés or use as a filling for dainty sandwiches.

TEA, COCKTAIL OR WEDDING SANDWICHES

Each of the following spreads makes about 1 cup (250 grams) sandwich filling. Season mixture with salt and pepper to taste and moisten with mayonnaise. Spreads containing onion are excellent for cocktail canapés; keep fillings well-seasoned but "onionless" for tea and wedding sandwiches.

1. Combine 3 Hard-Boiled Eggs (page 16), shelled and chopped, ¼ cup (30 grams) each minced radish and cucumber, 2 tablespoons (15 grams) each chopped parsley and sweet pickle, 1 tablespoon (8 grams) minced chives.

2. Combine 3 Hard-Boiled Eggs (page 16), shelled and chopped, ¼ cup (30 grams) chopped ripe, green or stuffed olives and 2 tablespoons (15 grams) each chopped celery and parsley.

3. Combine 3 Hard-Boiled Eggs (page 16), shelled and chopped, 2 tablespoons (15 grams) each minced pimento, celery and green pepper or capsicum.

4. Combine 3 Hard-Boiled Eggs (page 16), shelled and chopped, ¼ cup (30 grams) each chopped, seeded tomato and cucumbers.

5. Combine 3 Hard-Boiled Eggs (page 16), shelled and chopped, ¼ cup (60 grams) minced ham, chicken, tongue or flaked cooked fish, 1 tablespoon (8 grams) each minced scallions or spring onions, chopped pickle and parsley.

DEVILED EGGS

12 Hard-Boiled Eggs (page 16),
   shelled
½ cup (125 grams) Mayonnaise (page
   207)
Dash of dry mustard
Salt to taste
3 dashes Tabasco or another hot
   pepper sauce

1 tablespoon (8 grams) each minced
   dill pickle, pimento-stuffed olives,
   capers and chives
Pimento and parsley clusters for
   garnish

Halve eggs lengthwise and remove yolks. Cut a thin slice from underside of each egg-white half to balance it on the plate.

Make a very smooth paste of the yolks, mashing well with a fork or pressing through a sieve. Combine with remaining ingredients except the garnish.

Spoon yolk mixture into egg whites, piling high in center; better still, press mixture through a pastry bag fitted with a large fluted tube (it's easy and fun).

Cut pimento into 12 long thin strips. Curl a strip on top of each egg to look like a tiny red rose and insert stem of a sprig of parsley on one side.

Arrange eggs on serving platter, cover with plastic wrap or foil and refrigerate until ready to serve. Makes 24 half eggs.

Variations: Add any of the following ingredients to yolk mixture when making deviled eggs: deviled ham, mashed tuna fish or salmon, grated onion, ground ham, grated Parmesan cheese, toasted sesame seeds, finely chopped nuts or finely chopped fresh tarragon or dill.

HUNGARIAN STUFFED EGGS

12 Hard-Boiled Eggs (page 16),
   shelled
3 tablespoons (45 grams) mayonnaise
3 tablespoons (45 grams) commercial
   sour cream
1 tablespoon (15 grams) prepared
   mustard

2 scallions or spring onions including
   green tops, minced
1 teaspoon (5 milliliters) Worcestershire sauce
Cayenne, salt and paprika to taste

Slice eggs lengthwise and carefully remove yolks from whites.

Mash yolks with remaining ingredients and pile back into egg whites, mounding them up well in center. Sprinkle with paprika. Cover with plastic wrap or foil and chill until time to serve. Serves 8 or 12.

CRAB-STUFFED EGGS

12 Hard-Boiled Eggs (page 16), shelled
1 cup (250 grams) cooked flaked crabmeat
1 cup (125 grams) finely chopped celery

2 tablespoons (15 grams) minced green pepper or capsicum
1 tablespoon (15 milliliters) French Dressing (page 208)
⅓ cup (75 grams) commercial sour cream

Slice eggs in half lengthwise. Remove yolks and mash thoroughly.

Combine yolks, crabmeat, celery, green pepper, French Dressing and sour cream, mixing well.

Refill egg whites, cover with plastic wrap or foil and chill until serving time. Makes 24 half eggs.

GOOD-EGG DIP

1½ tablespoons (22 milliliters) lemon juice
1 tablespoon (15 milliliters) onion juice
2 teaspoons (10 grams) prepared mustard
Dash of hot pepper sauce
½ teaspoon (1 gram) salt

White pepper to taste
½ cup (125 grams) Mayonnaise (page 207)
6 Hard-Boiled Eggs (page 16), shelled
1 4-ounce (125-gram) package pimento cream cheese, softened
Parsley for garnish

In mixer or electric blender combine juices, mustard, hot pepper sauce, salt, pepper and Mayonnaise. Add eggs, one by one, beating or blending after each addition until mixture is smooth and light. Beat in cream cheese.

Spoon mixture into bowl and garnish with parsley sprigs. Serve with assorted chips, cocktail biscuits and crackers, or raw vegetable sticks. Makes about 2 cups (½ liter) dip or enough to serve 4 to 6.

Note: If desired, use chive cream cheese or Boursin cheese instead of the pimento cream cheese.

EGG AND OLIVE DIP

½ cup (125 grams) Mayonnaise (page
207)
1 tablespoon (15 milliliters) lemon
juice
Dash of hot pepper sauce
12 pimento-stuffed green olives, finely
chopped

6 Hard-Boiled Eggs (page 16), shelled
and chopped
1 4-ounce (125-gram) package onion-
flavored cream cheese
Parsley for Garnish

Combine Mayonnaise, lemon juice, hot pepper sauce and olives and beat until smooth.

Add eggs and beat until mixture is light and fluffy. Beat in cream cheese.

Spoon into a bowl and garnish with parsley. Serve with assorted chips, cocktail biscuits and crackers, or with thin slices of cucumber, zucchini or courgette. Makes about 2 cups (½ liter).

CURRIED EGG DIP

8 Hard-Boiled Eggs (page 16), shelled
and riced
1½ cups (375 grams) commercial
sour cream
2 tablespoons (15 grams) finely
chopped onion
1 teaspoon (5 grams) curry paste*

¼ cup (30 grams) chopped parsley
2 teaspoons (10 milliliters) lemon
juice
Dash of cayenne pepper
3 drops hot pepper sauce, or to taste
Salt to taste

* Curry paste may be purchased at stores carrying Indian foods or may be made by combining 1 tablespoon (2 grams) good curry powder and 2 tablespoons (30 milliliters) chicken broth in a small saucepan and stirring over low heat for about 2 minutes, or until mixture becomes a smooth paste. Will keep in a covered jar in refrigerator for months.

Combine all ingredients and beat until smooth. Chill until ready to serve.
Serve with assorted crackers and potato chips. Makes about 3 cups (¾ liter).

Note: If, after refrigerating, the dip is too firm, add a few drops of hot water and beat to desired consistency.

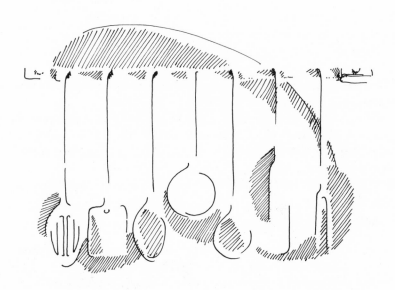

PICKLED EGGS

1 cup (¼ liter) white vinegar
½ cup (125 milliliters) water or beet or beetroot juice
1 tablespoon (2 grams) mixed pickling spices

1 teaspoon or 24 peppercorns
½ teaspoon (1 gram) salt
1 clove garlic
6 Hard-Boiled Eggs (page 16), shelled

In saucepan combine vinegar, water or beet juice, spices, peppercorns, salt and garlic. Bring to a boil and simmer for 10 minutes.

Place Hard-Boiled Eggs in bowl or jar and cover with the spiced vinegar. Cover bowl or jar and refrigerate for 24 hours before serving. Eggs may be kept in refrigerator for a week to 10 days. To serve, cut into wedges and arrange on serving plates. Serves 6.

First-Course Appetizers

As you will see, many of the first-course recipes can be used for party hors d'oeuvres.

EGGS À LA RUSSE

8 Hard-Boiled Eggs (page 16), shelled
1 cup (250 grams) Mayonnaise (page 207)
3 tablespoons (45 grams) chili sauce
1 tablespoon (8 grams) chopped green olives
2 tablespoons (15 grams) chopped chives

1 tablespoon (8 grams) each chopped parsley and minced scallions or spring onions
Juice of ½ lemon, or to taste
Pimento for garnish

Cut eggs in half lengthwise and arrange, cut-side down, in serving dish. To make Russian dressing combine remaining ingredients and pour over eggs. Garnish with strips of pimento. Chill until ready to serve. Serves 4 to 8.

EGGS REMOULADE

8 Hard-Boiled Eggs (page 16), shelled
1 cup (250 grams) Mayonnaise (page 207)
1 teaspoon (5 milliliters) lemon juice
1 clove garlic, minced
1 tablespoon (8 grams) finely chopped fresh tarragon or dash of dried

1 teaspoon (5 grams) Dijon mustard
1 tablespoon (8 grams) minced parsley
1 anchovy fillet, mashed
Watercress or parsley for garnish

Slice six of the eggs lengthwise and arrange on serving plate, cut-side down. Combine remaining ingredients. Chop remaining eggs finely and stir into sauce mixture. Pour sauce over eggs and chill. Garnish with watercress or parsley before serving. Serves 6.

EGGS CRESSONNIÈRE

Hard-boil 6 eggs (page 16); shell and cut in half lengthwise. Arrange cut-side down in serving dish and cover generously with Watercress Mayonnaise (page 205). Cover with plastic wrap or foil and refrigerate until ready to serve. Serves 6.

EGGS ANDALOUSE

Hard-boil 12 eggs (page 16). Remove shells and cut in half lengthwise. Arrange cut-side down in a serving dish and cover generously with Sauce Andalouse (page 208). Garnish with strips of pimento and capers. Cover with plastic wrap or foil and refrigerate until ready to serve. Serves 12.

EGGS RISSOLES

6 Hard-Boiled Eggs (page 16), shelled and finely chopped
6 medium mushrooms, chopped and sautéed in butter

¾ cup (180 milliliters) Béchamel Sauce (page 200)
Pastry for a Two-Crust Pie (page 159)
Shortening or oil for deep frying

Combine eggs, mushrooms and sauce.

Roll out pastry thinly on lightly-floured pastry cloth or clean tea towel and cut into rounds about 2½ inches (6 centimeters) in diameter.

Put 1 tablespoon (8 grams) egg mixture on one side of each pastry round. Moisten edges of pastry with water, fold pastry over filling and press edges together carefully to seal well.

When ready to cook, fry in deep oil heated to 365° F. (185° C.) for about 8 minutes, or until golden. Drain on absorbent paper and serve hot. Serves 6.

SWISS TARTS

¼ cup (30 grams) grated onion
1 tablespoon (15 grams) butter
½ pound (250 grams) Swiss cheese, shredded
3 eggs, beaten

1½ cups (375 milliliters) heavy or thick cream
Dash each dry mustard and cayenne
1 teaspoon (2 grams) salt
Cream Cheese Pastry (see below)

Sauté onion in butter until transparent. Mix onion with cheese.

In a large mixing bowl combine eggs, cream, mustard, salt and cayenne. Beat in onion-cheese mixture. Set aside.

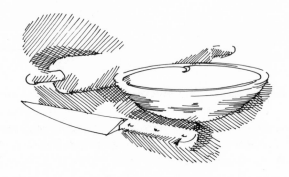

CREAM CHEESE PASTRY FOR INDIVIDUAL TART SHELLS

1 cup (250 grams) butter
6 ounces (180 grams) cream cheese
2 cups (200 grams) flour

Cream together butter and cream cheese; work in flour. Chill if very soft. This recipe will make either 48 cocktail-size tarts or 12 first-course appetizer tarts.

To make cocktail-tart shells: Roll pastry into 48 balls and press each over bottom and sides (up to top) of small 1¾-inch (4-centimeter) muffin or tart tins.

To make first-course tarts: Roll out half the pastry at a time on lightly-floured pastry cloth or clean tea towel and cut into 12 6-inch (15-centimeter) circles. Line 12 small tart tins about 3½ inches (9 centimeters) in diameter. Trim and flute edge as for any one-crust pie shell.

Set tins on baking sheets and fill two-thirds full of cheese filling. Bake in a preheated 350° F. (180° C.) oven for 20 minutes for cocktail tarts; 30 minutes for appetizer tarts. Serve warm from oven.

SPANAKOPETES (Greek Spinach-and-Egg Pie)

2 pounds (1 kilogram) fresh spinach, steamed and finely chopped
2 tablespoons (30 milliliters) olive oil
1 small onion, minced
½ cup (60 grams) minced parsley
½ pound (250 grams) feta or pot cheese

6 eggs, slightly beaten
Salt and pepper to taste
½ pound (250 grams) phyllo pastry (12 sheets)
½ pound (250 grams) butter, melted

Drain liquid from spinach and squeeze dry with hands. Set aside.

In a heavy frying pan heat olive oil and sauté onion until golden in color. Mix with parsley, cheese, eggs, salt and pepper. Stir in spinach and mix well.

Brush a 13 x 9-inch (32 x 32-centimeter) baking dish with melted butter. Cover dish with one sheet phyllo pastry, letting it hang over sides. Brush generously with butter. Repeat layering and buttering with phyllo pastry until there are five layers. Spoon in spinach mixture and smooth it over the pastry. Cover with remaining sheets of phyllo, brushing each well with butter and melting more butter if necessary.

With a sharp knife, cut off any surplus pastry around edges of dish. Bake in a preheated 375° F. (190° C.) oven for 45 minutes, or until golden brown.

Remove from oven and cool slightly. With a sharp knife cut into squares, 1½ inches (4 centimeters) in size for cocktail hors d'oeuvres, 3 inches (7.5 centimeters) in size for first-course appetizers. Makes 12 first-course appetizers; 48 hors d'oeuvres.

BUCKWHEAT BLINIS

---

1 cup (¼ liter) milk
½ yeast cake (15 grams) or ½ package (3.5 grams) active dry yeast
4 eggs, separated
½ teaspoon (1 gram) salt
1 teaspoon (5 grams) sugar

3 tablespoons (45 grams) melted
 butter
1½ cups (150 grams) sifted buck-
 wheat flour
Red caviar
Commercial sour cream

Scald milk and cool to lukewarm. Add yeast and stir until yeast is softened and combined with the milk.

In small mixing bowl beat egg yolks until thick and pale in color. Stir in yeast mixture, salt and sugar. Set bowl in a saucepan of warm water, cover and let batter rise until double in bulk, or for about 1½ hours.

Beat egg whites until stiff and fold gently but thoroughly into batter.

Preheat a pancake griddle or frying pan and butter it lightly. Cook blinis, using one spoonful batter for each cake, until golden brown on both sides, turning once. Keep griddle lightly buttered at all times. Serve with red caviar and commercial sour cream. Makes about 16 small blinis.

CHILES RELLENOS CON QUESO
(Green Peppers Stuffed with Cheese)

---

12 long, slim pale-green peppers or
 capsicums (or canned poblano
 peppers)
1 pound (500 grams) semi-soft cheese,
 such as Monterey Jack or Bel
 Paese

Flour, enough to coat peppers
6 eggs, separated
6 tablespoons (36 grams) flour
Vegetable oil for frying
Commercial sour cream

If using fresh peppers, put peppers on baking sheet and roast in a preheated 500° F. (260° C.) oven for 10 minutes. Remove from oven and wrap in a towel for 15 minutes to let peppers steam, then carefully peel off thin outer skin. With either canned or fresh peppers, slit peppers close to stem end and, leaving stem attached, discard seeds. Rinse out insides and set peppers aside.

Cut cheese into 12 long strips, 3 x 3 x ½ inches (7 x 7 x 1 centimeters). Insert one strip into each pepper. Chill thoroughly.

When ready to cook, roll stuffed peppers in a little flour.

Beat egg yolks until thick and pale in color. Beat egg whites until stiff and fold into egg yolks. Carefully fold in the 6 tablespoons of flour. This makes a very thick, fluffy batter.

Heat ½ to 1 inch (2.5 centimeters) oil in a small fry pan to 370° F. (190° C.). Place a spoonful of egg batter about ½-inch (1-centimeter) thick and 2-inches (5-centimeters) wide on a plate. Place a stuffed chili lengthwise on the mound and cover with more batter on top. Slide batter-coated pepper into the hot oil; sauté for 3 or 4 minutes or until golden brown, turning once with two slotted spoons or spatulas. Drain on paper toweling and keep warm in low oven until all are cooked.

Serve hot with commercial sour cream. Serves 6.

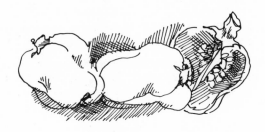

CHILI PUFF

3 3-ounce (90-gram) cans chopped green chilies, drained
1 pound (500 grams) Monterey Jack or mild Cheddar cheese, shredded

6 eggs, separated
1 cup (250 grams) commercial sour cream

Butter a 13 x 9-inch (32 x 22-centimeter) baking dish. Cover bottom with half the chilies and sprinkle with half the cheese. Cover with remaining chilies and sprinkle with remaining cheese.

Beat egg whites until stiff. Beat egg yolks until thick and beat in sour cream. Fold yolks and whites together and pour over chili-cheese mixture.

Bake in a 350° F. (180° C.) oven for 50 to 60 minutes. Serve hot and puffed. Serves 4.

EGGS DE MA MÈRE JEANETTE

6 Hard-Boiled Eggs (page 16), shelled
¾ cup (90 grams) minced parsley
4 cloves garlic, minced
½ cup (125 milliliters) heavy or thick
    cream
Salt and pepper to taste

1 teaspoon (5 grams) Dijon mustard
1 tablespoon (15 milliliters) wine
    vinegar
¼ to ½ cup (60 to 125 milliliters)
    olive oil
2 tablespoons (30 grams) butter

Cut eggs in half crosswise and turn yolks into a bowl. Set whites aside. Mash yolks thoroughly with a fork and stir in parsley, garlic, cream and salt and pepper. Work to a smooth paste.

Fill whites level with the yolk mixture, cover with plastic wrap or foil and chill until ready to cook.

To leftover egg-yolk mixture remaining in bowl (about 2 tablespoons or 30 grams), add mustard and vinegar and beat well. Use a wire whisk if possible or a wooden spoon. Continue to whisk while gradually adding the oil, drop by drop, so the yolk mixture thickens into a sauce the consistency of mayonnaise. Correct seasoning with salt and pepper and let remain at room temperature.

To cook the eggs: Heat butter in a fry pan until hot enough to sizzle a drop of water. Place stuffed eggs in the hot butter, yolk-side down, and cook over moderate heat until brown on underside. Cook, shaking pan and turning eggs from one side to the other, until warmed through.

Arrange eggs on warm serving platter and coat with the egg-yolk sauce. Serves 4.

This recipe is a favorite of Jacques Pépin and named for his mother.

MEATLESS EGG ROLLS

24 Egg-Roll Skins (recipe follows)
5 ounces (150 grams) water chestnuts,
    chopped
2 cups (500 grams) canned bamboo
    shoots, diced
4 scallions or spring onions, chopped
1 cup (125 grams) chopped celery
4 Hard-Boiled Eggs (page 16), shelled
    and chopped

½ teaspoon (1 gram) salt or to taste
2 tablespoons (30 milliliters) soy sauce
2 eggs, lightly beaten
1 tablespoon (6 grams) flour
2 tablespoons (30 milliliters) water
Cooking oil for frying
Dry mustard

Make Egg-Roll Skins and keep moist.

In mixing bowl combine water chestnuts, bamboo shoots, onions, celery and Hard-Boiled Eggs.

Add salt, soy sauce, and eggs and mix well.

Combine flour and water in a small container. Place about 2 tablespoons (15 grams) filling on each Egg-Roll Skin; brush edge of skin all around with flour mixture. Fold in two sides, then roll into a small cylinder. Press the flap edge lightly against the roll to seal it.

To cook: Pour cooking oil to the depth of about 1 inch (2.5 centimeters) in a deep frying pan and heat to 365° F. (185° C.). Fry a few egg rolls at a time in the hot oil for about 3 minutes, or until crisp and brown on all sides, turning once.

Drain on absorbent paper and keep warm in a 250° F. (120° C.) oven until ready to serve. Serve with Chinese mustard, made by mixing dry mustard with enough water to make a thick paste. Makes 24 egg rolls.

Note: Egg rolls traditionally contain either seafood or meat. If desired, 1 cup (250 grams) chopped cooked shrimp or prawns, chicken or flaked crabmeat may be substituted for the Hard-Boiled Eggs.

EGG-ROLL SKINS

2 cups (200 grams) flour
2 cups (½ liter) water

4 eggs
1 teaspoon (2 grams) salt

In mixing bowl or blender container combine flour, water, eggs and salt to make a thin batter. Pour batter into a small pitcher and stir occasionally.

Heat a small frying or crepe pan and brush lightly with butter. Pour in about 2 tablespoons (30 milliliters) of the batter and *immediately* raise pan above the heat and, at the same time, tip it over the pitcher, rotating pan so the bottom becomes covered with a thin layer of batter and any excess drains back into the pitcher. Sounds hard, but it is really easy.

The heat of the pan will dry the layer of batter. Shake the finished skin out onto a long sheet of waxed paper. Repeat, first heating the pan again thoroughly. Arrange cooked skins side by side on the paper.

When all skins have been cooked, place another sheet of waxed paper over them and roll the skins in the papers. They will stay moist this way until ready to fill or to freeze. Makes about 36 skins.

BLINTZES

8 ounces (250 grams) cottage or ricotta cheese	Salt to taste
4 ounces (125 grams) finely chopped toasted almonds	12 Egg-Roll Skins (page 117)
2 egg yolks	1 egg white, beaten
	¼ cup (60 grams) butter
	Commercial sour cream for garnish

In mixing bowl combine cheese, almonds, egg yolks and salt.

Place a spoonful of the cheese mixture in center of each skin. Fold sides over and roll. Seal edge with a little beaten egg white. Chill until ready to cook.

To cook: Heat butter in a fry pan. Place blintzes in it and sauté over low heat until browned on both sides. Serve hot with sour cream. Makes 12.

Note: 2 tablespoons (15 grams) chopped chives or parsley may be substituted for the almonds. This blintze recipe can also be used for a blintze dessert, accompanied by fresh berries or peaches.

GNOCCHI PARISIENNE

These delicate little dumplings are another delectable first-course appetizer.

4 tablespoons (60 grams) butter
1 cup (¼ liter) water
Salt and cayenne to taste
1 cup (100 grams) flour
Dash of dry mustard
4 tablespoons (30 grams) grated Parmesan cheese

4 eggs
Hot melted butter and additional grated Parmesan, or 2½ cups (625 milliliters) Mornay Sauce (page 200)

In a small saucepan combine the 4 tablespoons butter, water, salt and cayenne. Bring slowly to a boil.

Meanwhile combine the flour, mustard and 4 tablespoons grated cheese.

When liquid is boiling rapidly, dump in flour mixture all at once and, stirring rapidly with a wooden spoon, raise pan a few inches above the heat and continue to stir for 30 seconds or until paste comes away from sides of pan and forms a rough dough in the center.

Beat in eggs, one at a time, beating vigorously after each addition; after the last one, the paste will be very glossy. This may be done with an electric mixer if you wish.

To cook the gnocchi: Measure 4 quarts (4 liters) water into a large pan or kettle, and bring to a boil. Spoon the paste into a pastry bag fitted with a large plain pastry tube (No. 12). When water is boiling reduce heat so it barely simmers. Hold the bag over the water and press out the paste. As the paste is extruded, cut off 1-inch (2.5-centimeter) lengths with a knife, letting them drop into the simmering water. They will sink to the bottom, but as they puff and cook will rise to the surface and float. Cook the gnocchi for about 15 minutes, or until firm, constantly spooning the hot water over them so that they remain moist on all sides.

With a slotted spoon lift the gnocchi out of the simmering water onto paper toweling to drain. Then arrange them in a buttered baking dish, cover with waxed paper and refrigerate until time to serve.

Discard waxed paper from surface of the gnocchi and sprinkle generously with hot melted butter. Sprinkle again with grated Parmesan cheese, place under broiler or grill heat about 6 inches (15 centimeters) from source of heat and cook until nicely brown. Or pour the Mornay Sauce over them and bake in a preheated 350° F. (180° C.) oven for 15 to 20 minutes, or until sauce is bubbling hot. Serves 6.

EGGS IN ASPIC (Oeufs en Gelée)

One of the most elegant of all cold first-course appetizers is Eggs in Aspic. Served with a delicious egg sauce, it is as lovely to look at as it is to eat.

1 quart (1 liter) Quick Aspic (recipe follows)
12 fresh tarragon leaves or truffle cut-outs
6 Eggs Mollet (page 29), shelled and chilled

2 tablespoons (15 grams) chopped parsley
Lemon wedges for garnish
Aurora Sauce (page 206)

Make the aspic. Have it cold, but still liquid. Pour a thin layer into bottom of six egg ramekins or 6-ounce (180-gram) custard cups and chill until set.

Dip tarragon leaves into boiling water to wilt them, remove leaves from stems, dip into liquid aspic and use to decorate the bottom of the aspic-coated containers. Or use truffle cut-outs. Cover decoration with another thin layer of aspic and chill again.

Place an egg in each cup, fill half with still liquid aspic and chill. When set, fill cups with aspic and chill again until ready to serve. Pour remaining aspic into a bowl or cup and chill.

To serve: Run tip of a knife around egg between aspic and side of container. Dip container up to the rim in a bowl of lukewarm water and invert eggs one at a time onto a serving dish. They should slip out quite easily. If not, repeat the dipping.

Empty reserved aspic out onto a chopping board and sprinkle with parsley. Chop at all angles with a large wet chopping knife until aspic looks like shimmering diamonds. Surround eggs by a wreath of the chopped aspic and garnish platter with lemon wedges. Serve with Sauce Aurora. Serves 6.

QUICK ASPIC

3 cups (¾ liter) chicken broth
1 cup (¼ liter) tomato juice
4 envelopes (30 grams) plain
    gelatin
1 teaspoon (5 grams) sugar

Salt and freshly ground pepper to
    taste
2 egg shells, crushed
2 egg whites, lightly beaten
2 tablespoons (30 milliliters) Cognac

Combine all ingredients, except Cognac, in a large saucepan and bring slowly to a boil, stirring constantly, until mixture boils up in pan. Remove from heat, add 2 ice cubes and the Cognac.

Strain through a sieve lined with moist flannel or doubled cheesecloth. Strained aspic will be clear and golden. Makes about 1 quart (1 liter).

EGGS CHAUD-FROID

4 Coddled or Poached Eggs (pages 30
    and 21), chilled
½ envelope (4 grams) unflavored
    gelatin
1 tablespoon (15 milliliters) cold
    water
1 cup (¼ liter) hot Quick Aspic (see
    preceding recipe)

1 cup (¼ liter) Medium Cream Sauce
    or Mayonnaise (pages 197 and
    207)
Salt and white pepper to taste
2 black olives
Watercress and lemon wedges for
    garnish

Arrange eggs on a wire rack set over a baking sheet.

Soften gelatin in cold water, then stir in 2 tablespoons (30 milliliters) of the hot aspic to dissolve the gelatin. Stir into the Medium Cream Sauce or Mayonnaise and season to taste with salt and pepper. Let remaining aspic cool.

Spoon a little of the sauce over each egg and chill until set. Add a second layer of sauce and chill.

Garnish with cut-outs of black olives dipped in a little aspic. Cover the garnish with a coating of liquid aspic and chill until ready to serve. Chill remaining aspic.

To serve: Chop reserved aspic. Arrange eggs in a circle on a serving platter and fill center with chopped aspic. Garnish with watercress and lemon wedges. Serves 4.

EGGS AND SHRIMP IN ASPIC

1 pound medium-sized shrimps or prawns (500 grams) cooked, shelled and chilled
3 tablespoons (45 milliliters) heavy or thick cream
1 tablespoon (15 grams) mayonnaise
6 cooked artichoke bottoms
6 Poached Eggs (page 21), trimmed and chilled
1 quart (1 liter) Quick Aspic (page 121)
Radish roses, lemon wedges and watercress for garnish

Cut 6 shrimps in half lengthwise and set aside for garnish.

Dice 6 shrimps and set aside. Mince remaining shrimps and mash with the heavy cream and mayonnaise. Fold diced shrimp into the minced mixture.

Arrange artichoke bottoms on a baking tray and spread with the minced shrimp mixture. Top each with a Poached Egg.

Coat eggs and artichoke bottoms with two layers of cool, but still liquid,

Quick Aspic, chilling between each coating until set. Garnish each egg with two half shrimps dipped in aspic, placing them crosswise over the egg. Chill and coat several times more with aspic, chilling between each coating.

Chill, then dice, remaining aspic. Arrange eggs in a circle on a platter and fill center with diced aspic. Garnish with radish roses, lemon wedges and watercress. Serves 6.

6
Egg Dishes for the Convalescent

When we are ill or convalescing, we usually don't feel like eating. It makes good sense, then, to consider foods that offer the most in the way of nutrition in easily digested form. And that means eggs. They furnish more nutrients per calorie than any other single food except milk; they include all vitamins except C; and they contain 13 minerals—iron among them. No wonder our grandmothers combined these two natural foods in eggnogs to serve recuperating patients. And so this chapter opens with the time-honored eggnog. The wine may be omitted if you wish, but even my grandmama, who was a teetotaler, approved of sherry.

CONVALESCENT'S EGGNOG

1 egg or 2 egg yolks
2 teaspoons (10 grams) sugar
1½ ounces (45 milliliters) sherry or
    Madeira (optional)

1 cup (¼ liter) whole milk
Nutmeg

Put all ingredients except nutmeg into blender container. Cover and blend on medium speed until frothy. Pour into a tall glass and grate a little nutmeg on top. Serves 1.

A HONEY OF A DRINK

1 cup (¼ liter) milk

1 egg

2 tablespoons (30 milliliters) honey

Put all ingredients into blender container. Cover and blend on medium speed until frothy. Pour into a tall glass. Serves 1.

FRUIT AND EGG MIX-UP

1 cup (¼ liter) milk

1 egg

2 tablespoons (30 grams) sugar

¼ cup (60 milliliters) apple, orange or cranberry juice

Put all ingredients into blender container. Cover and blend on medium speed until frothy. Pour into a tall glass. Serves 1.

BANANA CUSTARD FROSTED

1 cup (¼ liter) milk

1 egg

1 scoop vanilla ice cream

1 banana

Pour milk into blender container. Add egg and ice cream. Cover and blend on high speed. Remove cover and, with motor on, slice in banana. Pour into large glass. Serves 1.

Variation: 1 large scoop Frozen Custard (page 134) may be used in place of the egg and vanilla ice cream.

APRICOT FROSTED

½ cup (125 milliliters) apricot nectar

½ cup (125 milliliters) milk

1 egg

1 scoop vanilla ice cream or Mint Sherbet or Sorbet (page 136)

Combine all ingredients in blender container. Cover and blend on medium speed until frothy. Pour into large glass. Serves 1.

Variation: To make a Prune Frosted, use prune juice and Lemon Sherbet or Sorbet (page 136) in place of the apricot juice and Mint Sherbet.

EGG CHOWDER

6 tablespoons (90 grams) butter
1 cup (125 grams) chopped onion
3 cups (500 grams) raw potato slices,
    ¼-inch (5-milliliters) thick
Salt to taste
Water

1 quart (1 liter) milk
1 cup (¼ liter) heavy or thick cream
6 Hard-Boiled Eggs (page 16), shelled
    and sliced
Oyster crackers

In large heavy saucepan melt 4 tablespoons (60 grams) butter and sauté onion until transparent and golden. Add potato, salt and enough water to just cover vegetables. Bring to a boil and simmer until potato slices are tender but not mushy.

Add milk and cream and heat to serving temperature. Add remaining 2 tablespoons (30 grams) butter and stir gently until butter is melted.

To serve: Arrange a sliced egg in bottom of each soup plate and ladle hot soup mixture over. Serve with oyster crackers. Makes enough for 6 servings.

GARLIC EGG SOUP

This soup is surprisingly delicious and delicate. The trick to keeping the garlic flavor from being overwhelming is to cook the garlic gently over low heat until golden, but without letting it burn.

8 cloves garlic
¼ cup (60 milliliters) olive oil
1 quart (1 liter) beef consommé

Salt and pepper to taste
6 sprigs watercress
6 raw eggs

Chop garlic finely and stew gently in olive oil for 5 minutes, or until pale golden color, watching it carefully.

Add consommé and bring to a boil. Add salt and pepper to taste.

Break an egg into each soup plate and add a sprig of watercress. Strain the boiling hot consommé over the egg and serve immediately. Serves 6.

CHICKEN NOODLE SOUP

3- to 4-pound (1½- to 2-kilogram)
    chicken, ready to cook
3 quarts (3 liters) water
2 teaspoons (4 grams) salt
1 onion, peeled and quartered
1 carrot, scraped and cut into quarters
Freshly ground black pepper

1 bay leaf
Small bunch parsley
Pinch thyme
4 ounces (125 grams) fine egg noodles
2 Hard-Boiled Eggs (page 16), shelled
    and chopped

In large saucepan put chicken, water, salt, vegetables, pepper, bay leaf, parsley stems and thyme. Bring to a boil, lower heat and poach chicken for 2 hours, or until very tender.

Strain chicken broth into a clean saucepan. Discard bones and skin of chicken, chop chicken meat and return meat to broth.

Add noodles, bring broth to a boil, and simmer for 5 to 6 minutes, or until noodles are tender.

Correct seasoning with salt and pepper, skim off any excess fat from surface, and add eggs. Sprinkle each serving with a little chopped parsley. Serves 6 to 8.

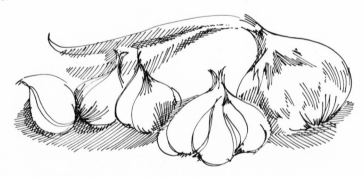

CREAM OF FRESH ASPARAGUS SOUP

1 bunch (1 pound or 500 grams) fresh
    asparagus
2 tablespoons (30 grams) butter
1 medium onion, chopped
1 quart (1 liter) chicken broth
Salt and pepper to taste

Pinch mace
1 tablespoon (15 milliliters) lemon
    juice
2 egg yolks
1 cup (¼ liter) heavy or thick cream

Snap off and discard tough white portions of asparagus. With a vegetable peeler, strip stalks to remove any sand that may be lurking beneath leaf scales. Soak in cold water 5 minutes. Drain, cut off tips and reserve. Cut remaining stalks into 1-inch (2.5-centimeter) lengths.

In heavy saucepan melt butter and sauté onion for 5 minutes. Add asparagus stalks and chicken broth. Season to taste with salt, pepper and mace. Bring to a boil and simmer over low heat for 30 minutes.

Meanwhile, put tips into small saucepan, cover with boiling water and simmer for 10 minutes. Set aside for garnish.

Force cooked asparagus stalks and liquid through a food mill or puree 2 cups (½ liter) at a time in electric blender. Return to heat.

In a medium-sized bowl combine lemon juice, egg yolks and cream with a little of the hot soup. Pour into remaining soup and cook for 2 minutes, stirring rapidly and being careful not to let it boil. Garnish each portion with a few asparagus tips. Serves 6.

CREAM OF SPINACH SOUP

1 pound (454 grams) fresh spinach	Salt and pepper to taste
¼ cup (30 grams) minced onion	1 cup (¼ liter) heavy or thick cream
¼ cup (60 grams) butter	2 egg yolks
2 cups (½ liter) chicken broth	

Wash and pick over spinach. Discard heavy stems. Drain well and shred leaves thinly.

In saucepan sauté onion in butter for a few minutes, until onion is transparent but not brown. Add spinach and cook for 5 minutes, stirring occasionally, until spinach is wilted. Add chicken broth, salt and pepper, bring to a boil and then simmer for 10 minutes. At this point, soup may be pureed in an electric blender if desired. It is also excellent left as it is with the shreds of spinach in the broth.

In a bowl combine cream, egg yolks and ½ cup (125 milliliters) of the hot soup. Remove soup from heat and gradually stir in egg mixture. Return soup to heat and cook for 2 to 3 minutes, stirring rapidly and being careful not to let it boil. Serves 4.

EGG AND LEMON SOUP

1 quart (1 liter) rich chicken stock	2 eggs
½ cup (125 grams) raw rice	Juice of 1 large lemon

In saucepan bring chicken broth to a boil. Add rice and simmer for 20 minutes, or until rice is tender.

Remove broth from heat and wait for it to stop boiling.

In a small bowl beat eggs thoroughly. Gradually beat in lemon juice. Beat in a little of the hot broth, then slowly stir egg mixture into the hot broth. Return soup to heat and cook for 3 minutes, stirring vigorously and being very careful not to let the soup boil. Serves 4.

CHICKEN ROYALE

6 tablespoons (90 grams) butter	½ cup (125 milliliters) heavy or thick
1 cup (125 grams) sliced fresh mush-	cream
rooms	4 egg yolks
6 tablespoons (36 grams) flour	4 chicken breast halves (750 grams),
2 cups (½ liter) hot milk	poached and cut into large
1 teaspoon (2 grams) salt or to taste	chunks
Dash cayenne pepper	Parsley for garnish
Sherry to taste (optional)	

In heavy saucepan melt butter and sauté mushrooms for 5 minutes. Stir in flour. Remove saucepan from heat and add hot milk. Return to heat and cook, stirring rapidly, until sauce is smooth and thickened. Blend in salt and cayenne and cook over low heat for 10 minutes, stirring occasionally. Add sherry.

In a small bowl combine cream and egg yolks with a little of the hot sauce. Gradually stir into remaining sauce. Add chicken and cook over low heat for 3 minutes, stirring constantly. Do not let sauce boil.

Serve on buttered toast triangles, in Individual Tart Shells (page 112) or with cooked rice. Garnish with parsley. Serves 4.

CINNAMON FRENCH TOAST À LA MODE

1 teaspoon (5 grams) brown sugar
Dash of cinnamon
1 egg
2 tablespoons (30 milliliters) milk

1 slice white, raisin or whole wheat
    bread
1 tablespoon (15 grams) butter
Vanilla ice cream

In small bowl combine brown sugar, cinnamon, egg and milk. Beat with a fork or rotary beater until well blended and pour into a shallow pan or pie dish.

Put the bread slice in the egg mixture and let it stand for about 30 seconds. Turn bread over and let it stand a few minutes longer.

Melt butter in a frying pan and when it begins to foam place the soaked bread slice in it and cook until nicely browned on the bottom, about 3 minutes. Turn with a pancake turner and cook the second side for 3 minutes or until nicely browned.

Transfer bread to a serving plate and top with a scoop of vanilla ice cream. Serves 1.

BAKED CUSTARD

---

4 eggs
½ cup (125 grams) sugar
3 cups (¾ liter) hot milk

1½ teaspoons (7 milliliters) vanilla
essence
Nutmeg (optional)

Beat eggs and sugar together until well blended. Gradually stir in hot milk. Stir in vanilla. Pour into six 6-ounce (180-gram) custard cups or a 1½-quart (1½-liter) casserole. Sprinkle with nutmeg.

Set custard cups or casserole in a large baking pan and set pan on rack in oven. Pour very hot water into pan to within ½ inch (1 centimeter) of top of custard.

Bake in preheated 350° F. (180° C.) oven for 25 to 30 minutes for custard cups; 35 to 40 minutes for casserole. Remove immediately from hot water. Serve warm or chilled. Serves 6.

BAKED ORANGE CUSTARD
WITH ORANGE SAUCE

---

6 eggs, lightly beaten
¾ cup (180 grams) sugar
2 cups (½ liter) whole milk, scalded
1 tablespoon (8 grams) grated orange
   rind

4 teaspoons (20 grams) cornstarch or
   cornflour
1½ cups (375 milliliters) orange juice

Combine eggs with ½ cup (125 grams) sugar and gradually stir in the hot milk. Stir in orange rind. Pour mixture into six 6-ounce (180-gram) custard cups. Set cups in baking pan and pour hot water into pan to reach within ½ inch (1 centimeter) of top of custard in cups.

Bake in preheated 325° F. (170° C.) oven for 35 to 40 minutes, or until knife inserted halfway between center and outside edge comes out clean.

Remove custard immediately from the hot water and place on wire rack to cool.

Meanwhile, in small saucepan blend remaining ¼ cup (60 grams) sugar with cornstarch. Slowly stir in orange juice. Bring mixture to a boil and cook over moderate heat for 1 minute, stirring constantly. Remove from heat to cool.

Turn custard from cups into serving plates and serve with the orange sauce. Serves 6.

RICE PUDDING

4 eggs
2 cups (½ liter) milk
½ cup (125 grams) sugar
1 tablespoon (15 grams) butter,
    melted
2 teaspoons (10 milliliters) vanilla
    essence

2 cups (500 grams) cooked rice
⅓ cup (40 grams) golden raisins or
    sultanas, optional
Cinnamon or nutmeg, optional

In medium-sized bowl beat eggs and blend in milk, sugar, butter and vanilla. Stir in rice and raisins, if desired.

Bake in a preheated 325° F. (170° C.) oven for 35 minutes. Stir gently to redistribute rice through liquid and continue to bake for 20 to 25 minutes longer, or until a knife inserted halfway between center and outside edge comes out clean. Sprinkle with cinnamon or nutmeg, if desired. Serves 6 to 8.

TAPIOCA PUFF

3 cups (¾ liter) milk
½ cup (125 grams) sugar
¼ cup (45 grams) quick-cooking
    tapioca
3 eggs, separated

1½ teaspoons (7 milliliters) vanilla
    essence
Dash of cream of tartar

In medium-sized saucepan stir together milk, sugar and tapioca. Let stand for 5 to 10 minutes.

In small mixing bowl beat egg yolks until thick and pale in color, about 5 minutes. Stir yolks into milk mixture. Cook, stirring constantly, over medium heat until mixture thickens; simmer for about 15 minutes. Remove from heat. Stir in vanilla. Set aside.

In large mixing bowl beat egg whites and cream of tartar until eggs are stiff but not dry. Gently fold in tapioca mixture, leaving small puffs of egg white. Spoon into serving dishes and chill until firm, or for at least 2 hours. Serves 6.

FROZEN CUSTARD

6 eggs, lightly beaten
2 cups (½ liter) milk
¾ cup (180 grams) sugar
2 tablespoons (30 milliliters) honey
2 cups (½ liter) heavy or thick cream

1 tablespoon (15 milliliters) vanilla
essence
Crushed ice
Rock salt

In medium-sized saucepan blend eggs, milk, sugar and honey. Cook over low heat, stirring constantly, until mixture thickens and just coats a metal spoon. Do not let it boil. Cool, cover and refrigerate until very cold.

When ready to freeze, combine chilled custard, cream and vanilla. Pour into 1-gallon (4-liter) ice-cream freezer container and freeze according to manufacturer's directions, using six parts ice to one part rock salt. Makes ½ gallon (2 liters).

Here are some other delicious variations to try:

Chocolate
Add 3 squares or 3 ounces (90 grams) unsweetened chocolate to egg-milk mixture. Cook, cool and freeze as above.

Strawberry
Omit vanilla essence from custard. Cook and cool as above. Partially freeze. Add 2 cups (454 grams) sweetened crushed fresh strawberries, and finish freezing as above.

Banana Nut
Mash 3 large ripe bananas. Stir bananas and ½ cup (60 grams) chopped toasted pecans into custard mixture. Freeze as above.

SHERRY PARFAIT

---

1 cup (250 grams) sugar
1 cup (¼ liter) dry sherry
8 egg yolks, lightly beaten

3 cups (¾ liter) heavy or thick cream,
    whipped

Combine all ingredients and chill thoroughly. When ready to freeze, pour into a 1-gallon (4-liter) ice-cream freezer container and freeze according to manufacturer's directions, using six parts ice to one part rock salt.

Remove dasher, repack container with ice and salt and let the parfait ripen for 2 hours before serving. Makes 2 quarts (2 liters).

THREE-IN-ONE SHERBET OR SORBET*

1½ cups (375 grams) sugar
3 cups (¾ liter) water or cranberry
    juice
3 large ripe bananas, sliced
1-pound can (454 grams) crushed
    pineapple in own juice

½ cup (125 milliliters) lemon juice
1 cup (250 milliliters) orange juice
3 egg whites

In large saucepan combine sugar and water or cranberry juice. Bring to a boil and simmer for 5 minutes, or until all the sugar is dissolved. Cool, then chill.

---

* These three sherbets can be made in refrigerator ice-cube trays if you do not have an ice-cream freezer. Follow basic recipes, making syrup and cooling same. As soon as syrup is cool, pour it into refrigerator trays and freeze for about 1 hour or until syrup turns to mush. Transfer mush to a bowl and beat until fluffy. Continue with basic recipe. Beat egg whites, add whites to beaten mush and turn back into refrigerator trays and freeze until solid.

Pour chilled mixture into ice-cream freezer container and add fruit and fruit juices.

Beat egg whites until stiff but not dry. Add to freezer container, cover and churn together, following manufacturer's directions. Makes 3 quarts (3 liters).

MINT SHERBET OR SORBET*

1½ cups (375 grams) sugar
4 cups (1 liter) water
2 cups (250 grams) fresh mint leaves, shredded

1 cup (250 milliliters) lemon or lime juice
4 egg whites, stiffly beaten

In large saucepan combine sugar and 2 cups (½ liter) of the water. Bring to a boil and simmer for 5 minutes, stirring, until sugar is dissolved. Add mint leaves to the boiling syrup, cover and cool, then chill.

Pour chilled mixture into ice-cream freezer container, add remaining ingredients and churn together, following manufacturer's directions. Makes 2 quarts (2 liters).

LEMON SHERBET OR SORBET*

1½ cups (375 grams) sugar
1 cup (¼ liter) water
¾ cup (180 milliliters) lemon juice
2 teaspoons (4 grams) grated lemon rind

4 cups (1 liter) water
2 egg whites, beaten until stiff but still glossy

In saucepan combine sugar and water, bring slowly to a boil and simmer for 3 minutes or until sugar is dissolved. Cool, then chill.

Pour chilled mixture into ice-cream freezer container, add remaining ingredients and churn together, following manufacturer's directions. Makes 2 quarts (2 liters).

7
Egg Breads

Eggs add richness and a golden hue to countless breads, rolls, muffins and coffee cakes. For example, the famous French brioche and the traditional egg breads and rolls of many countries all over the world would not be possible were it not for the contribution that eggs make to their texture, flavor and nutrition. On the following pages is a variety of breads that I hope you will enjoy.

FRENCH TOAST IN A HURRY

1 tablespoon (15 grams) butter	2 slices bread
1 egg	Syrup, jam or confectioners or icing
1 tablespoon (15 milliliters) milk	sugar and a lemon wedge

Melt butter in a 10-inch (25-centimeter) frying pan over moderately high heat until just hot enough to sizzle a drop of water.

Meanwhile, beat egg and milk with a fork in a pie dish until well blended. Dip bread slices into the egg mixture, turning to coat evenly.

Place bread slices in the hot butter, reduce heat to moderate and cook until lightly browned. Turn and brown other side. Transfer to serving plate. Serve with syrup, jam or sugar and lemon. Serves 1.

COLD-OVEN POPOVERS (The Poppingest Ever!)

There's a lot of hocus-pocus about making a popover pop. In reality there is no mystery to it. You don't need any special recipe; you don't have to preheat your oven or use special cast-iron pans. One basic recipe works for every-one. The trick is to use ordinary 6-ounce (180-gram) Pyrex custard cups set wide apart on a baking sheet and to make four popovers instead of six or eight from the recipe. This means filling the cups three-fourths full of batter.

2 eggs	1 cup (¼ liter) milk
½ teaspoon (1 gram) salt	1 level cup (100 grams) flour

Butter four 6-ounce (180-gram) custard cups generously.

If you have an electric blender, put eggs, salt, milk and flour (no need to sift) into container in order given; otherwise measure them into a mixing bowl. Blend or beat until batter is smooth. In the blender, it is usually neces-sary to stop once and stir mixture down from sides with a rubber spatula.

Pour batter into prepared cups, set wide apart on a baking sheet, filling cups three-fourths full. Set baking sheet in a cold oven until ready to bake— and this means next morning, if you wish, for the batter can sit in the oven overnight without any harm coming to it.

When ready to bake, turn oven to 450° F. (230° C.) and bake popovers for 30 minutes. Toward end of baking time, but not before, check popovers and if they are becoming too brown, turn temperature down to 400° F. (200° C.) and bake for another 5 minutes or until popovers are crisp. Serves 4. Recipe may be doubled.

YORKSHIRE PUDDING

The batter for Yorkshire Pudding is exactly the same as a popover batter, but it is baked in roast beef drippings and becomes a main course "pudding." To many it is a favorite accompaniment to roast beef.

To bake, pour ¼ cup (60 milliliters) beef drippings into a 13 x 9 x 2-inch (32 x 22 x 5-centimeter) baking or roasting pan and heat until nearly smok-ing. Pour in popover batter and bake in a preheated 450° F. (230° C.) oven for 10 minutes. Reduce heat to 375° F. (190° C.) and bake for 15 minutes longer. Cut into squares and serve immediately. Serves 6 to 9.

If it is necessary to hold Yorkshire Pudding for any length of time, reduce heat to 250° F. (120° C.). It will stay puffed and crisp for another 20 minutes.

VIRGINIA LAPLAND CAKES

Pinch of salt
1 cup (100 grams) flour

3 eggs, separated
1 cup (¼ liter) heavy or thick cream

Generously butter one dozen medium-sized muffin or baking-powder cake tins. Add salt to flour.

In a large mixing bowl beat egg whites until stiff but not dry. With the same beater, in another bowl, beat egg yolks thoroughly. In a third bowl beat cream until stiff. Fold flour mixture into egg yolks alternately with the whipped cream. Fold in egg whites.

Spoon batter into prepared muffin tins using about two rounded spoonfuls per cup and bake in a preheated 375° F. (190° C.) oven for 20 to 25 minutes or until puffed and lightly brown. Makes 12 muffins.

Note: With the simple addition of 4 teaspoons (20 grams) baking powder to the flour and salt in the foregoing recipe, the batter may be cooked in a preheated waffle iron according to manufacturer's directions. Chill the batter for 30 minutes before cooking. These are called Dutch Cream Waffles.

NORWEGIAN PANCAKES

1 cup (250 grams) commercial sour
    cream
1 cup (250 grams) small-curd cottage
    cheese
4 eggs

¾ cup (75 grams) sifted flour
1 tablespoon (15 grams) sugar
½ teaspoon (1 gram) salt
Butter and syrup to taste

Combine sour cream and cheese. Beat in eggs one at a time. Stir in remaining ingredients and beat with mixer or electric blender until well blended.

Bake on a hot greased griddle until bubbles break on surface. Turn with spatula and continue to cook until golden brown. Serve with butter and syrup. Makes 24 4-inch (10-centimeter) pancakes.

Blueberry Pancakes

Add to batter 1 cup (150 grams) blueberries or blackberries, fresh or frozen.

Apple Pancakes

Add to batter 1½ cups (250 grams) finely diced raw apple.

FLUFFY EGG DUMPLINGS

1-pound (454 grams) loaf white bread
¼ cup (60 milliliters) water
6 eggs
½ cup (60 grams) finely chopped
    parsley

½ cup (60 grams) minced onion
Salt to taste
Dash of nutmeg

Trim crusts from bread and reserve for another dish; or scatter for the birds. Crumb the rest of the bread a few slices at a time in an electric blender or rub through a coarse sieve.

Sprinkle bread crumbs with water and toss lightly with a fork.

Beat eggs and add to the crumbs. Toss again. Add parsley, onion, salt and nutmeg. Mix well.

Drop by spoonfuls on top of a bubbling stew or a fricassee. Cover container tightly and let the dumplings steam for 30 minutes. They will puff and be very light. Makes 12 medium-sized dumplings.

BANANA BREAKFAST BREAD

2 cups (200 grams) sifted flour
⅔ cup (150 grams) sugar
1 tablespoon (15 grams) baking powder
1 teaspoon (2 grams) salt
½ cup (60 grams) chopped nuts

3 tablespoons (45 grams) butter
3 eggs, beaten
1 cup (180 grams) mashed ripe bananas (about 2)
⅓ cup (75 milliliters) milk

Sift flour, sugar, baking powder and salt into a large mixing bowl. Stir in nuts.

Melt butter. Combine eggs, bananas, milk and melted butter. Add liquid all at once to flour mixture and stir until batter is smooth.

Oil a 9 x 5-inch (22 x 12-centimeter) bread loaf tin. Turn batter into loaf pan and bake in a preheated 350° F. (180° C.) oven for 1 hour, or until a wooden toothpick inserted in center comes out clean. Cool on wire rack for 10 minutes before removing from pan. Makes 1 large loaf.

BUTTERMILK DOUGHNUTS

4 cups (400 grams) flour (sifting not necessary)
1½ teaspoons (7 grams) baking or bicarbonate of soda
1½ teaspoons (7 grams) cream of tartar
1 teaspoon (2 grams) salt

3 eggs
1 cup (250 grams) sugar
4 tablespoons (60 grams) melted butter
1 cup (¼ liter) buttermilk
Shortening or oil for deep frying

Combine flour, baking soda, cream of tartar and salt.

In large mixing bowl beat eggs thoroughly. Gradually beat in sugar. Stir in melted butter and buttermilk. Add flour mixture and mix thoroughly, adding a little more flour if necessary to make a very light, sticky dough. Chill.

Turn dough out on well-floured board and roll out ½-inch (1-centimeter) thick. Do not handle dough any more than necessary. Dough will be soft. Cut into doughnuts with floured cutter and let stand for 30 minutes before frying.

Fry a few at a time in deep fat heated to 375° F. (190° C.) for about 4 minutes, or until brown on both sides, turning once. Makes 2 dozen.

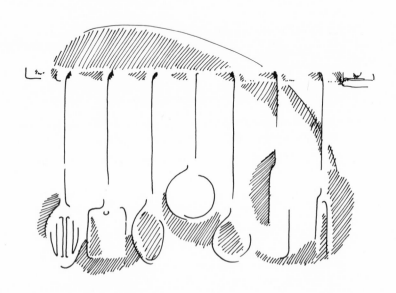

SWEET EGG ROLLS

1 teaspoon (5 grams) sugar	½ teaspoon (1 gram) salt
1 cake (30 grams) yeast or 1 envelope (7 grams) active dry yeast	2 tablespoons (30 grams) sugar
	5 to 6 cups (500 to 600 grams) flour
3 tablespoons (45 milliliters) luke-warm water	1 cup (250 grams) butter
	1⅓ cups (325 grams) sugar
1 cup (¼ liter) lukewarm milk	3 eggs

Put sugar in a large mixing bowl; add yeast and let soften in lukewarm water for 5 minutes, or until it becomes frothy. Add milk, salt, the 2 tablespoons sugar and 1 cup (100 grams) flour. Stir to mix well and let stand for 20 minutes.

In a small bowl cream together half the butter (125 grams) and the 1⅓ cups sugar until soft and fluffy. Add to yeast batter. Beat in eggs, one at a time. Stir in 4 cups (about 400 grams) flour to make a soft sticky dough. Cover and let rise for 1½ hours. Meanwhile, melt remaining butter and set aside to cool.

Punch dough down and turn out on floured board. Knead, adding more flour, about 1 cup (100 grams) to make a dough that is still very soft, but not sticky.

Shape dough into 18 rolls about 2 inches (5 centimeters) in diameter. Pour half the melted butter into a 14 x 8½ x 2-inch (35 x 20 x 5-centimeter) baking tin. Place rolls of dough close together on the baking tin and let rise for 1 hour, or until double in bulk.

Pour remaining butter over tops of rolls and bake in a preheated 375° F. (190° C.) oven for 20 minutes. Makes 18 rolls.

SALLY LUNN BREAD

---

1 cup (¼ liter) hot milk	1 cake (30 grams) yeast or 1 envelope
¾ cup (180 grams) butter	(7 grams) active dry yeast
¼ cup (60 grams) sugar	4 cups (400 grams) flour
1½ teaspoons (3 grams) salt	4 eggs

In a large mixing bowl combine hot milk, butter, sugar and salt. Stir until butter is melted and mixture is lukewarm.

Stir in yeast and let stand for 5 minutes to proof.

Beat in 2 cups (200 grams) flour. Stir in eggs. Add another cup (100 grams) flour and beat until batter is smooth and elastic. With hands, knead in remaining flour, or enough to make a dough that is soft but not sticky. Cover and let rise in a warm place for 1½ hours.

Punch dough down, turn out on floured board and knead until smooth and elastic. Put dough in a well-oiled 10-inch (25-centimeter) tube pan or 3- to 4-quart (3- to 4-liter) mold. Cover and let rise in a warm place for about 1 hour or until doubled.

Bake in a preheated 375° F. (190° C.) oven for 40 to 45 minutes, or until golden brown. Remove from pan immediately and cool on a wire rack. Serve warm with butter and jam. Makes 1 large loaf.

SPOON BREAD

---

4 eggs, separated
2 cups (½ liter) milk
3 tablespoons (45 grams) butter
1 cup (150 grams) cornmeal

1 teaspoon (5 grams) baking powder
½ teaspoon (1 gram) salt
Dash of cream of tartar

In a large mixing bowl beat egg whites until stiff. Set aside.

In a small mixing bowl beat egg yolks at high speed until thick and lemon-colored, about 5 minutes. Set aside.

In large saucepan over moderate heat combine milk and butter. Cook, stirring, until butter melts. Stir in cornmeal, baking powder and salt. Cook, stirring constantly until mixture thickens, about 3 minutes. Remove from heat and beat in egg yolks.

Gently fold cornmeal mixture and cream of tartar into egg whites. Pour batter into an oiled 1½- to 2-quart (1½- to 2-liter) casserole.

Bake in a preheated 375° F. (190° C.) oven for 30 to 35 minutes, or until a knife inserted halfway between center and outside edge comes out clean. Serve immediately. Serves 4 to 6.

RICH YEAST COFFEE CAKE

---

1 cake (30 grams) yeast or 1 envelope
    (7 grams) active dry yeast
¼ cup (60 milliliters) lukewarm water
4 cups (400 grams) flour
1 teaspoon (2 grams) salt
4 tablespoons (60 grams) sugar
1 cup (250 grams) butter
8 egg yolks
½ cup (125 milliliters) lukewarm milk

¼ cup (60 grams) melted butter
1 cup (125 grams) chopped blanched
    almonds
1 cup (250 grams) light brown sugar
Confectioners or icing sugar to frost
    top (optional)
Candied fruit and blanched almonds
    for decoration (optional)

Soften yeast in the lukewarm water. Set aside.

In large mixing bowl combine flour, salt and sugar. Add butter and work into flour with tips of fingers until finely crumbled. Add yeast mixture and egg yolks and mix well to a fairly stiff dough. Add milk and mix again thoroughly. Turn out on floured board and knead until dough is smooth and elastic.

Roll dough out on a floured surface into a long rectangle about 18 inches (45 centimeters) in length. Brush surface of dough with part of the melted butter, sprinkle with ·three-fourths of the nuts and the brown sugar. Roll dough lengthwise into a thick sausage and form into a circle. Press. ends firmly together and transfer to a 10- or 12-inch (25- to 30-centimeter) cake tin, brushed with remaining melted butter.

With kitchen scissors, cut deep slanting slashes about halfway through the roll at intervals of about 2 inches (5 centimeters).

Let coffee cake rise in a warm place for about 1 hour, or until puffed and doubled in bulk.

Bake in a preheated 350° F. (180° C.) oven for 40 minutes, or until golden brown.

Remove from pan while warm to a cake rack to cool. While still warm, if desired, frost top with confectioners or icing sugar and decorate with candied fruits and remaining blanched almonds. Makes 1 large coffee cake.

BRIOCHES OR BRIOCHE EGG BREAD

This is the most exquisite bread in the world. Although not the traditional recipe for brioche, it is my favorite because it is so easy to make and is every bit as good, shaped either into the familiar fluted buns with their saucy caps on top, or baked in loaves. The baked bread remains good in the freezer for at least six months and makes delicious toast and sandwiches.

1 cup (250 grams) butter

2 cakes (60 grams) yeast or 2 envelopes (14 grams) active dry yeast

½ cup (125 milliliters) lukewarm
water

1 teaspoon (5 grams) sugar

½ teaspoon (1 gram) salt

¼ cup (60 grams) sugar

6 whole eggs

4–4½ cups (about 450 grams) flour

Use an electric mixer if possible. Soften butter to room temperature. Soften yeast in the lukewarm water with the 1 teaspoon sugar until it froths.

In mixing bowl put the salt, the ¼ cup sugar and the eggs. Beat with rotary beater or at high speed until eggs are very fluffy and sugar and salt are dissolved.

Beat in 2 cups (200 grams) flour, then stir in yeast.

Divide butter into chunks and add to yeast mixture. Add another cup (100 grams) flour and beat well. Work in 1 more cup (100 grams) or enough to make a soft dough that doesn't stick to the hands. Be careful when adding the last amount of flour not to add more than is absolutely necessary.

Turn dough out onto floured board and knead until dough is smooth and satiny. Cover with a towel and let rise for 1½ hours.

Turn dough out again on lightly floured board and knead again briefly before shaping into brioches or loaves.

To make brioches: Oil two dozen fluted brioche tins. Roll dough into a long sausage about 1-inch (2.5-centimeters) thick. Cut off pieces of dough and form into balls the size of walnuts. Make smaller balls of dough for the "heads" or "caps" of the brioches. Make a deep indentation in the top of each of the large balls and insert the smaller ball into the hole. Place each brioche in an oiled tin, place tins on baking sheets and let bread rise in a warm place for 30 minutes, or until well puffed. Bake in a preheated 350° F. (180° C.) oven for 15 to 20 minutes. Remove immediately from tins to cool on wire racks. Makes 18 brioches.

To make loaves: Oil two loaf pans. Cut dough into two equal parts. Knead each part briefly and shape into a thick loaf. Put loaves into the oiled pans, cover with a towel, and let rise for about 45 minutes, or until well rounded in pans. Bake in a preheated 375° F. (190° C.) oven for 45 to 50 minutes. Makes two loaves.

For a glazed surface: Before baking, brush brioches or loaves with a mixture of one egg yolk or whole egg beaten with 1 tablespoon (15 milliliters) water.

Note: This dough may be kept in the refrigerator for several days and baked when needed. Keep it in a bowl covered with plastic wrap. Refrigerated dough will take at least twice as long to rise as freshly made.

To reheat frozen brioches: Pop the frozen brioches, sprinkled with a little water, into a Brown-In-Bag or a brown paper bag and bake in a 300° F. (150° C.) oven for 30 minutes.

Brioche Melba Toast

The best thing you could put in your mouth! Bread should be a little stale or slightly frozen. Slice very thin and arrange on a baking sheet. Brush with melted unsalted butter and bake in a 300° F. (150° C.) oven for 30 minutes or until golden. Turn off oven and let toast become dry and crisp.

Toasted Breads
to Accompany Eggs

ROUND CROUTONS

The word "crouton" is a fancy name for thinly sliced bread cut into shapes and fried or baked.

For Round Croutons: Cut large circles from bread with a large cookie or biscuit cutter and arrange in a frying pan in a few tablespoons of hot, foaming butter. Cook over moderate heat. As soon as the croutons are golden brown, turn and sauté the other side, adding a little more butter if necessary. Remove from fry pan and keep warm on absorbent paper until ready to use. Croutons can also be prepared by frying them in deep fat, or buttering and baking them in a moderate oven, or by toasting and buttering them before serving.

SMALL CROUTONS

Small, crisp croutons make an attractive and different bed for a fried, soft-boiled or poached egg, and are a nice texture-touch to scrambled eggs or an omelet.

Trim crusts from bread and cut into strips ½-inch (1-centimeter) wide, then across in ½-inch (1-centimeter) pieces. Sauté the bread in hot melted butter, tossing constantly, until crisp and golden brown. Drain on absorbent paper.

GRILLED ENGLISH MUFFINS

Toasted English muffins make a good bed for almost any egg. For a change, try cooking them my way: Fork the muffins in half and butter each half liberally. Place on aluminum foil about 3 inches (7.5 centimeters) from broiler or grill heat and broil until butter is foamy and muffins are lightly browned. Watch carefully so they do not burn.

CROUSTADES

These are "bread boxes" that may vary in size and shape. Remove the crusts from a day-old loaf of unsliced bread. To make a square-shaped crous-tade: Slice bread about 2-inches (5-centimeters) thick and, with a small sharp knife, cut a square about ¼ inch (5 millimeters) from outside edge and re-move the center, leaving a base ¼-inch (5-millimeters) thick. To make a round-shaped croustade: Take a slice of bread and cut out a round about 2½ inches (6 centimeters) in diameter and remove same, leaving a round bread box.

Put the square or round bread boxes on a baking sheet, brush all sides with melted butter and toast in a preheated 300° F. (150° C.) oven for about 15 to 20 minutes, or until crisp and golden brown.

TOAST CUPS

Trim crusts from thinly sliced, firm-textured bread and brush one side of each slice with melted butter; press slices, buttered-side down, into muffin cups and brush inside with melted butter. Bake in a preheated 350° F. (180° C.) oven for 10 to 12 minutes or until golden brown. Remove from pans and use as shells for creamed or scrambled eggs.

8
The Wonderful World of Egg Desserts

Can you imagine what dessert making would be without eggs? There would be no pies, puddings, cakes, custards or cream puffs. As it is, there are so many desserts that two chapters are devoted to them in this book. This, the first, contains the old standbys such as baked custards, cream pies, sweet soufflés and omelets, mousses and parfaits—more than enough to satisfy anyone's sweet tooth, and elegant enough to impress gatherings of the most discriminating diners. More dramatic and fancier desserts are found in the next chapter.

POTS DE CRÈME AU VANILLE (Little Pots of Cream)

2 cups (½ liter) heavy or thick cream
3 tablespoons (45 grams) sugar
6 egg yolks

2 teaspoons (10 milliliters) vanilla essence

Heat cream and sugar until it simmers, stirring until sugar is dissolved.

Beat egg yolks lightly and gradually pour the hot cream over them, stirring vigorously. Stir in vanilla and strain mixture into small pottery pots or ramekins. Set containers in a shallow pan containing 1 inch (2.5 centimeters) hot water and bake in a preheated 325° F. (170° C.) oven for about 20 minutes, or until a knife inserted in the side of the cream comes out dry. Do not overbake. Better to have cream a little runny in the center than overbaked. Chill before serving. Makes 8 little pots.

Pots de Crème au Chocolat
   Substitute 4 ounces (125 grams) sweet (dark) chocolate for half the sugar.

Pots de Crème au Café
   Substitute 1 teaspoon (2 grams) instant coffee dissolved in 1 tablespoon (15 milliliters) of water for the vanilla.

CRÈME BRÛLÉE (Burnt Sugar)

One of the most elegant in the whole wide world of desserts is a rich, smooth custard with a crunchy topping of "burned" sugar. It is not difficult to make if directions are followed implicitly.

4 tablespoons (60 grams) sugar	3 cups (¾ liter) heavy or thick cream
1 tablespoon (15 grams) cornstarch or cornflour	2 teaspoons (10 milliliters) vanilla essence
7 egg yolks	1 cup (250 grams) light brown sugar

In an electric mixer or mixing bowl beat sugar and cornstarch into egg yolks. Continue to beat vigorously for 2 to 3 minutes, or until mixture is thick and pale in color.
   In heavy-bottomed 1½-quart (1½-liter) saucepan heat cream to a simmer. Gradually pour hot cream into egg-yolk mixture, beating constantly. Strain mixture back into the same saucepan.
   Cook over moderate heat, stirring rapidly with a wooden spoon and reaching all over bottom and sides of pan. As soon as bubbles begin to appear around edge of the cream it will increase in volume and rise up in the pan. Stir like mad and do not let it boil. Remove immediately from the heat and continue to stir vigorously to cool the cream and prevent further cooking. If it is not as thick as vanilla pudding, repeat this cooking and stirring once again.
   Stir in vanilla off the heat and pour cream into a pretty serving bowl. Chill for several hours or overnight if possible.
   To finish: Set serving bowl in a shallow pan containing cracked ice to pre-

vent the bowl cracking from sudden temperature change. Sprinkle brown sugar thickly and evenly over top of cream. Broil or grill 3 inches (7.5 centimeters) from source of heat for 4 to 5 minutes, or until sugar melts and caramelizes. Be careful not to let the sugar burn. Serve immediately, or chill again for several hours. Serves 6.

Note: In case of curdling—this can happen easily if you permit the cream to reach a boiling temperature—empty custard into blender container and blend until smooth. It will become thin but will thicken when chilled. It will never be quite as good as if this had not happened, but everyone except you will think it divine!

MEXICAN FLAN

3 tablespoons (45 grams) sugar
¾ cup (90 grams) blanched almonds
1⅓ cups (325 milliliters) condensed milk
¾ cup (180 milliliters) heavy or thick cream

3 eggs
3 egg yolks
Whipped cream (optional garnish)

Measure sugar into a 9-inch (22.5-centimeter) layer-cake tin. Place tin over direct heat and stir constantly with a wooden spoon until sugar melts and turns a dark caramel in color. Remove from heat immediately to cool and become brittle.

Grind nuts in an electric blender and leave in container. Add milk, cream, eggs and yolks. Cover and blend on high speed for 10 seconds.

Empty mixture into caramelized pan, set pan in a larger pan containing about ½ inch (1 centimeter) hot water and bake in a preheated 325° F. (170° C.) oven for 45 minutes or until set.

Cool, then refrigerate overnight.

To serve: Invert flan on serving platter and it will slip easily out of the pan. If desired, garnish or serve with whipped cream. Serves 6.

OEUFS À LA NEIGE (Snow Eggs)

2 cups (½ liter) milk	2 teaspoons (10 milliliters) vanilla
½ cup (125 milliliters) heavy or thick cream	4 egg whites
	Dash of cream of tartar
6 tablespoons (90 grams) sugar	4 egg yolks, lightly beaten

In large saucepan or 8-inch (20-centimeter) fry pan, combine milk, cream, 2 tablespoons (30 grams) of the sugar and the vanilla. Bring to a simmer.

Meanwhile, beat egg whites with the cream of tartar until stiff. Gradually beat in remaining sugar, 1 tablespoon (15 grams) at a time, until mixture is smooth, thick and glossy. Drop this meringue by large spoonfuls into the simmering milk and poach for about 5 minutes, turning each meringue over a couple of times as it poaches.

Remove poached meringues with slotted spoon to absorbent paper to drain.

Beat egg yolks with a little of the hot milk and gradually add to milk mixture, stirring rapidly. Stir over moderate heat until custard is thick enough to coat the spoon. Pour custard into serving dish and cool.

When cool, top the custard with the meringue "eggs" and refrigerate until ready to serve. Serves 8.

BAVARIAN CREAM (Basic Recipe)

1 envelope, or 1 tablespoon (8 grams), plain gelatin

2 tablespoons (30 milliliters) cold water

4 egg yolks

½ cup (125 grams) sugar

1 cup (¼ liter) hot milk

Flavoring (see below)

1 cup (¼ liter) heavy or thick cream, whipped

Fresh fruit for garnish or a dessert sauce (optional)

Soften gelatin in cold water.

In heavy saucepan beat egg yolks and sugar until mixture is smooth and creamy. Gradually stir in hot milk. Cook, over moderate heat, stirring constantly, until cream is smooth and thick enough to coat the spoon. Be careful the mixture does not boil.

Remove from heat, add gelatin and stir until gelatin is completely dissolved. Stir in one of the flavorings below and let cream cool, stirring occasionally to prevent a crust from forming.

When cold and thick, but before cream is completely set, fold in whipped cream. Pour into a 1-quart (1-liter) mold and chill until firm.

When ready to serve, run a silver knife around edge of cream, dip the mold in and out of hot-to-the-hand water and invert onto cold serving plate. Garnish with fruit to taste or serve with a favorite dessert sauce.

For different flavors, try any one of the following. They are *all* good. All recipes serve 4.

Vanilla Bavarian Cream
Add 1 teaspoon (5 milliliters) vanilla essence along with the gelatin.

Coffee Bavarian Cream
Add 1½ tablespoons (24 milliliters) coffee extract with the gelatin. Or add 1 teaspoon (2 grams) instant coffee dissolved in 1 tablespoon (15 milliliters) hot water.

Chocolate Bavarian Cream
Add 2 ounces (60 grams) unsweetened chocolate, melted, with the gelatin.

Liqueur Bavarian Cream
Stir in ¼ cup (60 milliliters) favorite liqueur just before folding in the whipped cream.

CHOCOLATE BREAD PUDDING

There is something quite heartwarming about an old-fashioned bread pudding.

12 to 15 slices French bread, each about ½-inch (1-centimeter) thick
3 tablespoons (45 grams) melted butter
4 ounces or squares (125 grams) sweet (dark) chocolate
2 cups (½ liter) milk

1 cup (¼ liter) light cream
3 eggs
3 egg yolks
½ cup (125 grams) sugar
1 tablespoon (15 grams) confectioners or icing sugar
Whipped cream (optional)

Brush both sides of the bread slices with melted butter, arrange on a baking sheet and bake in a 375° F. (190° C.) oven for 6 to 7 minutes or until lightly golden on one side; turn and bake 5 minutes longer or until brown on both sides. Remove bread from oven and arrange slightly overlapping on bottom of a 14 x 8-inch (35 x 20-centimeter) oval baking dish. Set aside.

Melt chocolate over low heat, stirring constantly.

In medium-sized saucepan heat milk and light cream to a simmer and stir in melted chocolate.

In large mixing bowl beat eggs, egg yolks and sugar until thoroughly blended. Stir in the chocolate milk. Pour the chocolate mixture over the toast. Set the dish in a large shallow roasting pan containing 1 inch (2.5 centimeters) boiling water.

Bake in a preheated 375° F. (190° C.) oven for 30 minutes. Just before serving, sprinkle with confectioners sugar. You may spoon whipped cream or English Custard Sauce (recipe follows) over each portion. Serves 8.

ENGLISH CUSTARD SAUCE

5 egg yolks
⅔ cup (150 grams) sugar
2 cups (½ liter) hot milk

2 tablespoons (30 milliliters) sherry or light rum

Combine egg yolks and sugar in a medium-sized saucepan. Beat well with rotary beater or whisk until thick and pale in color. Gradually beat in the hot milk. Cook, stirring constantly with a wooden spoon, making sure the spoon reaches all over bottom and sides of saucepan. Cook until custard is thick enough to coat the spoon. Do not let the sauce boil. As soon as bubbles appear around sides of pan and custard is slightly thickened, remove from heat. Continue to stir, or set the saucepan in a bowl of cold water to reduce the temperature and prevent further cooking.

Stir in sherry or rum and serve lukewarm or cold.

Makes enough for 8 sauce servings or about 3 cups (¾ liter).

ONE-CRUST PASTRY PIE OR TART SHELL
(Basic Recipe)

You only need to know how to make one type of pie crust or pastry—*the best*—which is known as Tart Paste or Pâte Sucrée. It's incredibly easy if you have a pastry cloth or a clean tea towel and a cloth stockinette for your rolling pin. The best part of this pastry is that you can use all the flour you need in rolling it out, and it won't hurt it at all. Chilling the dough for 30 minutes before rolling helps, but is not necessary once you learn how to handle the dough.

This basic recipe makes one 9-inch (22.5-centimeter) pie shell. You may double recipe.

1 cup (100 grams) flour (no need to sift)
1 egg yolk
1 tablespoon (15 grams) sugar (omit for savory pies)

½ cup (125 grams) cold butter (but not out of freezer), sliced
1 to 2 tablespoons (15 to 30 milliliters) water

Measure flour into a mixing bowl and make a well in the center. Into the well put egg yolk, sugar, butter and 1 tablespoon (15 milliliters) water. With a hand, knead these center ingredients, adding the other tablespoon of water if necessary, to make a smooth paste, and gradually work in the flour to make a dough that can be gathered together into a ball. Add a little more water if necessary.

Spread out a pastry cloth on work surface and rub generously with flour. Rub flour into a stockinette stretched on rolling pin. Press ball of dough into a flat circle with heel of hand and sprinkle lightly with flour.

Begin rolling dough out into a circle, rolling from center of dough to outer edge all around the circle. Turn the dough occasionally to keep both sides floured and to make sure it is not sticking to the cloth.

When pastry is ⅛-inch (3-centimeters) thick and 1½ inches (3.5 centi-meters) or more larger than pie dish or tart tin, place rolling pin in center and flip one side of dough over the rolling pin. Transfer pastry to pie dish by means of the rolling pin and fit it loosely into the dish. Trim off edge, leaving one-half inch (1 centimeter) overhanging. Fold overhanging edge back and under and build up a fluted rim: Place left forefinger against inside of pastry rim and pinch outside with right thumb and forefinger. Repeat all around edge.

Fill and bake according to directions given with each recipe.

To bake only shell: Prick bottom and sides of pastry generously with a fork and bake in a preheated 425° F. (220° C.) for 12 to 15 minutes. Should the pastry bubble or buckle, reach into the oven with fork in hand and pierce the bubble. It will deflate.

VANILLA CREAM PIE

3 tablespoons (45 grams) cornstarch
  or cornflour
½ cup (125 grams) sugar
¼ cup (60 milliliters) cold milk
1½ cups (375 milliliters) hot milk
½ cup (125 milliliters) heavy or thick
  cream
3 egg yolks, lightly beaten

1½ teaspoons (7 milliliters) vanilla
  essence
½ cup (125 milliliters) heavy or thick
  cream, whipped
1 9-inch (22.5-centimeter) baked Pie
  Shell (page 159)
Whipped cream for garnish

In heavy saucepan combine cornstarch and sugar. Stir in cold milk. Gradu-ally add hot milk and bring to a boil over moderate heat, stirring. Cook, stir-ring constantly, until mixture is thickened. Blend in cream, beaten lightly with egg yolks and a little of the hot milk mixture and cook over moderate heat for 2 minutes longer, stirring vigorously.

Remove from heat. Add vanilla and pour into baked pie shell. When filling is cool, garnish top of pie with whipped cream. Serves 6.

Chocolate Cream Pie

Follow recipe for Vanilla Cream Pie but add 2 ounces (60 grams) of semi-sweet (dark) chocolate to custard mixture.

BUTTERSCOTCH CREAM PIE

1½ cups (375 grams) light brown
    sugar, firmly packed
9 tablespoons (54 grams) flour
3 cups (¾ liter) hot milk
3 egg yolks, beaten
3 tablespoons (45 grams) butter

2 teaspoons (10 milliliters) vanilla
    essence
1 9-inch (22.5-centimeter) baked Pie
    Shell (page 159)
Whipped cream for garnish

In saucepan combine sugar and flour. Gradually stir in hot milk. Cook over low heat, stirring constantly, until thickened.

Blend in egg yolks and cook over low heat, stirring constantly, for 3 minutes longer. Remove from heat and add butter and vanilla. Cool slightly.

Pour into baked pie shell. When cool, if desired, top with whipped cream. Serves 6.

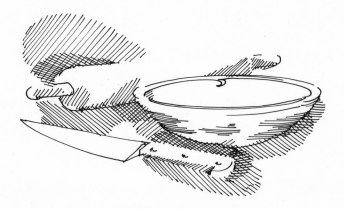

EGGNOG PIE

1 9-inch (22.5-centimeter) baked Pie
    Shell (page 159)
4 eggs, separated
½ cup (125 grams) sugar
1 envelope (8 grams) plain gelatin

1 cup (¼ liter) hot milk
1 cup (¼ liter) heavy or thick cream
2 tablespoons (30 milliliters) dark rum
Nutmeg

In medium-sized saucepan beat egg yolks and sugar until thick and pale in color. Stir in gelatin. Gradually stir in hot milk. Cook over moderate heat, stirring constantly, until custard is very hot and thickened. Do not let it boil.

Remove from heat and stir over cracked ice until mixture is cool and beginning to set.

Beat egg whites until stiff but not dry. Whip cream until light and fluffy. Fold egg whites and half the cream into the egg custard. Stir in rum. Spoon into pie shell. Decorate top of pie with remaining whipped cream and sprinkle with nutmeg. Chill. Serves 6.

LEMON OR LIME MERINGUE PIE

1 9-inch (22.5-centimeter) baked Pie
   Shell (page 159)
1 cup (250 grams) sugar
¼ cup (25 grams) flour
3 tablespoons (45 grams) cornstarch
   or cornflour
2 cups (½ liter) water
3 eggs, separated

2 tablespoons (30 grams) butter
¼ to ⅓ cup (60 to 75 milliliters)
   lime or lemon juice to taste
Grated rind of 1 lime or lemon
2 drops yellow or green food coloring,
   if desired
Dash of cream of tartar
6 tablespoons (90 grams) sugar

In medium-sized saucepan combine sugar, flour and cornstarch. Gradually stir in water. Bring to a boil and cook, stirring constantly, until thickened.

Gradually stir the hot mixture into the egg yolks, return to saucepan over low heat and cook, stirring, for 3 minutes.

Remove from heat and stir in butter, lemon or lime juice, grated rind and food coloring. Cool slightly, then pour into baked shell. Cool completely.

Make a 3-egg white Soft Meringue as follows: Beat 3 egg whites until frothy. Add dash of cream of tartar and continue to beat until egg whites are stiff enough to hold a peak. Gradually beat in 6 tablespoons (90 grams) sugar and beat until meringue is stiff and glossy. Pile meringue lightly on pie, making sure it touches edge of pastry so that the meringue won't shrink. With a spatula make large attractive swirls on top. Bake in a preheated 425° F. (220° C.) oven for 5 to 6 minutes or until the high peaks of the swirls are delicately tinged with brown. Serves 6.

LEMON OR LIME CREAM PIE

1 9-inch (22.5-centimeter) baked Pie
    Shell (page 159)
1 cup (250 grams) sugar
3 tablespoons (45 grams) cornstarch
    or cornflour
1 envelope (8 grams) plain gelatin
1 cup (¼ liter) water
6 egg yolks, beaten
2 tablespoons (15 grams) grated
    lemon or lime rind

¼ cup (60 milliliters) lemon or lime
    juice, or to taste
1 tablespoon (15 grams) butter
2 egg whites
3 tablespoons (45 grams) sugar
1 cup (¼ liter) heavy or thick cream,
    whipped
Shaved Chocolate Curls for garnish
    (recipe follows)

In medium-sized saucepan combine the 1 cup (250 grams) sugar, corn-starch and gelatin. Stir in water. Bring to a boil over medium heat, stirring constantly, and cook until thick and bubbling.

Slowly stir a small amount of the hot mixture into egg yolks, then stir egg yolks into hot mixture in saucepan and cook over low heat for 1 minute longer, stirring rapidly.

Remove custard from heat and stir in lemon or lime rind, juice and butter. Cool.

Beat egg whites to soft peaks. Beat in the 3 tablespoons (45 grams) sugar, one tablespoon (15 grams) at a time, and continue to beat until stiff.

Fold egg-yolk mixture gently into egg whites. Chill for 30 minutes, then fold in whipped cream.

Spoon into prepared pie shell and sprinkle with shaved chocolate. Serves 6.

SHAVED CHOCOLATE CURLS

Melt small amount of semi-sweet (dark) baking chocolate over very low heat, stirring until smooth. Immediately pour onto a hard flat surface, such as a baking sheet. With a thin metal spatula spread the melted chocolate to the thickness of a playing card, keeping it smooth. Chill in refrigerator or freeze. If work area is cool, this may not be necessary. Place sheet with chocolate on work surface. Select a sharp knife. Hold the knife at each end with both hands and work away from you, keeping the blade at a 45° angle. Now, slip the knife under the thin hardened chocolate layer, and, as you go, it will peel off in large decorative curls.

STRAWBERRY RUM CREAM TART

1 9-inch (22.5-centimeter) baked Pie
    Shell (page 159)
3 tablespoons (18 grams) flour
3 tablespoons (45 grams) sugar
1 egg
1 egg yolk
1 envelope (8 grams) plain gelatin
¾ cup (180 milliliters) hot milk
2 egg whites, stiffly beaten
½ cup (125 milliliters) heavy or thick
    cream, whipped

Dark rum
Fresh strawberries, hulled and sliced,
    for garnish
3 tablespoons (45 grams) currant jelly
    or jam
2 teaspoons (10 milliliters) water
Rosettes of Whipped Cream (page
    196) optional

In medium-sized saucepan combine flour, sugar, egg and egg yolk and beat until mixture is smooth. Stir in gelatin. Gradually pour in hot milk, stirring rapidly. Stir over low heat until mixture begins to simmer around edge, but do not let it boil.

Set saucepan in a bowl of cracked ice and stir until cream is thick and cool. Fold in egg whites, whipped cream and rum to taste.

Spread the rum cream in pie shell and cover the surface of the cream with sliced strawberries. In small saucepan combine jelly and water. Stir over low heat until jelly is melted. Brush over strawberries.

If desired, decorate with rosettes of whipped cream. Serves 6.

VANILLA SOUFFLÉ (Basic Recipe)

2 tablespoons (30 grams) butter
3 tablespoons (18 grams) flour
¾ cup (180 milliliters) hot milk
¼ cup (60 grams) sugar
4 egg yolks
2 teaspoons (10 milliliters) vanilla
    essence

5 egg whites
Confectioners or icing sugar to dust
    top
½ cup (125 grams) vanilla-flavored
    whipped cream

Butter a 1-quart (1- liter) soufflé dish and sprinkle inner surface with a little sugar.

In large saucepan melt butter and stir in flour. Cook, stirring, until mixture bubbles.

Remove saucepan from heat and add hot milk, all at once. Stir rapidly with wire whisk or wooden spoon until mixture is blended. Stir in sugar. Return to moderate heat and cook, stirring constantly, until sauce is smooth and very thick. Remove from heat and beat for 2 minutes until slightly cool.

Beat in egg yolks, one at a time. Stir in vanilla.

Beat egg whites until stiff but not dry. Stir about one-quarter of the beaten egg whites into the sauce. Then fold in remaining egg whites lightly and gently.

Turn soufflé mixture into prepared dish and set in the center of an oven preheated to 400° F. (200° C.). Immediately reduce oven temperature to 375° F. (190° C.) and bake for 30 to 35 minutes, or until soufflé is set. Sprinkle with confectioners or icing sugar before serving and serve with vanilla-flavored whipped cream. Serves 4.

Praline Soufflé

Add ½ cup (60 grams) Praline Powder (page 185) to basic Vanilla Soufflé before folding in egg whites.

Lemon Soufflé

Add finely grated rind of 1 lemon and 1 tablespoon (15 milliliters) lemon juice to basic Vanilla Soufflé before folding in egg whites.

Orange Soufflé

Add finely grated rind of half an orange and 3 tablespoons (45 milliliters) orange juice to basic Vanilla Soufflé before folding in egg whites.

Liqueur Soufflé

Omit vanilla in basic Vanilla Soufflé recipe and substitute 2 tablespoons (30 milliliters) Grand Marnier, Benedictine, curaçao, Cointreau or maraschino.

Peach Macaroon Soufflé

Soak ½ cup (60 grams) macaroon crumbs in 2 tablespoons (30 milliliters) Cognac. Combine with 1 cup (¼ liter) fresh peach puree. Stir into egg-yolk mixture before adding egg whites. Use a 1½-quart (1½-liter) dish. Serve with Cognac-flavored whipped cream.

Strawberry Soufflé

Combine 2 cups (375 grams) sliced fresh strawberries (1 pint or ½ liter), ½ cup (125 milliliters) orange juice and ½ cup (125 milliliters) orange curaçao. Sprinkle with 2 tablespoons (30 grams) sugar and set aside. Make basic soufflé. Drain excess juice from strawberries and reserve. Pour strawberries into bottom of a 1½-quart (1½-liter) soufflé dish. Pour soufflé mixture on top and bake according to recipe. Combine drained juice and whipped cream and serve as sauce.

Chocolate Soufflé

Increase sugar in basic recipe to ⅓ cup (75 grams). Melt 2 squares or ounces (60 grams) unsweetened chocolate with 2 tablespoons (30 milliliters) cold coffee, stirring until smooth. Fold into flour-milk mixture before beating in egg yolks.

SWEET FRENCH OMELET (Basic Recipe)

2 eggs for each omelet, beaten
1 tablespoon (15 grams) butter for each omelet
2 teaspoons (10 grams) sugar for each omelet

½ teaspoon (2 grams) finely granulated or castor sugar for each omelet

Follow basic recipe for a French Omelet (page 61). Heat butter in omelet pan and when hot pour in eggs beaten with the 2 teaspoons sugar for each omelet. Stir over brisk heat until eggs begin to thicken and set. Roll and turn out onto heatproof platter. Make the number of omelets needed, arranging them side by side on the platter.

Sprinkle each with finely granulated or castor sugar and glaze quickly under broiler heat or grill.

Chocolate Omelet

Make a Sweet French Omelet (preceding recipe), adding 2 squares or ounces (60 grams) melted semi-sweet (dark) chocolate to the egg-yolk mixture. Serve with slightly sweetened whipped cream.

Omelet au Rhum

Make individual Sweet French Omelets (page 166) but omit final glazing. Pour a jigger of warm rum over each omelet, light the rum and take omelet to table flaming. (Kirsch may be substituted.) If desired, garnish with sweetened sliced strawberries, raspberries or dark sweet cherries.

Jam Omelet

Some jams that make delicious fillings are apricot, blackcurrant, strawberry, raspberry and orange marmalade. Make a Sweet French Omelet (page 166) but, just before rolling, spread with jam. Then roll, turn out on serving plate and dust with finely granulated or castor sugar. Flame, if you wish, with a fruit-flavored brandy or liqueur.

Ginger Omelet

Make individual Sweet French Omelets (page 166), but, just before rolling, spread with 1 tablespoon (8 grams) chopped preserved ginger mixed with 2 tablespoons (30 grams) whipped cream. Surround by a ribbon of ginger syrup.

Fresh Fruit Omelet

Make Sweet French Omelets (page 166) for each person. Just before rolling, spread with sliced fruit or berries, sweetened to taste. Spread top with commercial sour cream and sprinkle with confectioners or icing sugar. Garnish with whole berries or slices of fruit.

FROZEN VANILLA MOUSSE (Basic Recipe)

6 egg yolks
½ cup (125 grams) sugar
1 cup (¼ liter) heavy or thick cream,
    lightly whipped

2 teaspoons (10 milliliters) vanilla
    essence

Beat egg yolks and sugar until very thick and pale in color. Fold in whipped cream and vanilla and beat over cracked ice until very frothy.

Pour into a 1-quart (1-liter) mold and freeze for several hours or until frozen through. Serves 4.

Try some of the following variations:

Coffee Mousse

Substitute 2 tablespoons (30 milliliters) very strong coffee for the vanilla.

Chocolate Mousse

Melt 4 ounces (125 grams) semi-sweet (dark) chocolate and stir into egg-yolk mixture.

Liqueur Mousse

Use 2 tablespoons (30 milliliters) favorite liqueur instead of vanilla: anisette, kirsch, maraschino are all good.

Fruit Mousse

Fold into egg-yolk mixture ½ cup (125 grams) fresh fruit puree.

FROZEN ORANGE MOUSSE

⅔ cup (150 milliliters) fresh orange
    juice
⅔ cup (150 grams) sugar

3 egg yolks
1 cup (¼ liter) heavy or thick cream,
    lightly whipped

In saucepan heat orange juice and sugar.

Beat egg yolks until thick and lemon-colored and stir into orange juice mixture. Cook over simmering water, stirring occasionally, until mixture coats the spoon. Remove from heat and cool thoroughly, stirring occasionally.

Fold in whipped cream. Pour into six 6-ounce (180-gram) individual fluted cups and freeze until firm. Serves 6.

CARIBBEAN MOCHA MOUSSE

8 ounces (250 grams) semi-sweet
  (dark) chocolate
4 tablespoons (60 milliliters) strong
  coffee

5 eggs, separated
2 tablespoons (30 milliliters) Jamaica
  rum
Whipped cream for garnish

In saucepan cook chocolate and coffee over low heat, stirring constantly, until chocolate is melted and mixture is smooth.

Beat egg yolks until thick and pale in color. Stir in chocolate and rum.

Beat egg whites until stiff and fold into chocolate mixture. Pour into six individual 6-ounce (180-gram) soufflé dishes or ramekins and chill for at least 3 hours. Serve topped with whipped cream. Serves 6.

REFRIGERATOR FRUIT MOUSSE (Basic Recipe)

Cold soufflés are really not soufflés. They are actually mousses set with gelatin in the refrigerator and *not* baked in the oven; nor do they rise in any mysterious way. Traditionally, they are served in a soufflé dish that is collared to allow the mixture to be piled above the edge of the dish, creating the illusion of a hot soufflé.

2 envelopes (15 grams) plain gelatin
Juice of 1 lemon
4 tablespoons (60 milliliters) water
5 eggs
4 egg yolks

½ cup (125 grams) sugar
Grated rind of 1 lemon
1 cup (250 grams) fresh fruit puree
Whipped cream and/or fresh fruit for
  garnish

In small saucepan soften gelatin in lemon juice and water. Stir over low heat until gelatin is thoroughly dissolved. Set aside.

In bowl of an electric mixer* combine whole eggs, yolks and sugar. Beat vigorously until egg mixture is very thick and pale in color. Beat in lemon rind.

Gradually beat in dissolved gelatin and fold in the fruit puree.

Pour into serving dish and refrigerate for 3 hours, or until set. Serve garnished with whipped cream and/or some fresh berries or slices of fruit. Serves 6.

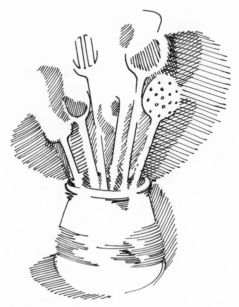

COLD LEMON SOUFFLÉ WITH RASPBERRY SAUCE AU KIRSCH

1 envelope (8 grams) plain gelatin
Grated rind of 4 lemons
½ cup (125 milliliters) lemon juice
¾ cup (180 grams) sugar
1 cup (250 milliliters) egg whites

1 cup (¼ liter) heavy or thick cream, whipped
Raspberry Sauce au Kirsch (recipe follows)

Tear a strip of aluminum foil that is a little longer than the circumference of a 1-quart (1-liter) soufflé dish. Fold the strip in half lengthwise and tie it

---

* Without an electric mixer, place mixing bowl over a saucepan containing hot water and beat with a rotary beater for about 5 minutes, or until thick and pale.

around the dish with a piece of string, letting the foil rise above the upper edge of the dish by 1½ inches (3 centimeters).

In a small saucepan combine the gelatin, lemon rind, lemon juice and sugar. Stir over low heat until gelatin and sugar are thoroughly dissolved and the liquid is clear. Chill for about 30 minutes, or to a syrupy consistency. It must be cold, but not cold enough to set.

Beat egg whites until stiff but not dry. Fold thoroughly into lemon mixture. Fold in whipped cream.

Spoon the mousse into the soufflé dish and chill until set.

When ready to serve, remove the collar and serve with Raspberry Sauce au Kirsch. If desired, garnish with thin slices of lemon or with rosettes of additional whipped cream. Serves 6.

Note: This dessert freezes very well. Defrost overnight in refrigerator or at room temperature for 4 hours before serving.

RASPBERRY SAUCE AU KIRSCH

1½ cups (360 grams) fresh raspberries	2 tablespoons (30 milliliters) kirsch
⅓ cup (75 grams) sugar	

In small saucepan combine raspberries and sugar and heat to simmering. Simmer for 10 minutes, then press through a fine sieve or blend in an electric blender and strain. Chill and stir in the kirsch. Makes about 1½ cups.

Note: A 10-ounce (300-gram) package of frozen raspberries may be substituted for the fresh raspberries and sugar.

FRENCH CUSTARD PARFAIT

A sinfully rich ice cream that does not form ice crystals when it freezes is known as a parfait.

½ cup (125 grams) sugar	2 teaspoons (10 milliliters) vanilla
¼ cup (60 milliliters) water	essence
Pinch cream of tartar	2 cups (½ liter) heavy or thick cream,
4 egg yolks	whipped

In a small saucepan combine sugar, water and cream of tartar. Bring to a boil and cook rapidly until syrup spins a light thread.

Beat egg yolks until frothy. Gradually beat in hot syrup and continue to beat until egg yolks are thick and pale in color.

Stir in vanilla. Fold in whipped cream. Spoon into refrigerator tray, cover with waxed paper and freeze for about 3 hours, or until frozen. Makes 1 quart (1 liter).

CHOCOLATE PARFAIT

6 ounces (180 grams) semi-sweet (dark) chocolate bits
2 tablespoons (30 milliliters) strong coffee
¼ cup (60 grams) sugar

½ cup (125 milliliters) water
4 egg yolks
2 cups (½ liter) heavy or thick cream, whipped

Melt chocolate with coffee over low heat, stirring until smooth. Set aside to cool.

In small saucepan combine sugar and water. Bring to a boil and boil rapidly for 3 minutes, until syrupy.

Beat egg yolks until frothy. Gradually beat in syrup and continue to beat until thick and pale in color. Fold in chocolate. Fold the chocolate mixture into the whipped cream.

Spoon into refrigerator tray, cover with waxed paper and freeze until firm. Makes 1 quart (1 liter).

BISCUIT TORTONI

⅓ cup (75 grams) sugar
2 tablespoons (30 milliliters) water
3 egg yolks
2 tablespoons (30 milliliters) sherry

1 cup (¼ liter) heavy or thick cream, whipped
4 tablespoons (30 grams) ground toasted almonds

In saucepan combine sugar and water. Bring to a boil and boil rapidly for 3 minutes, until syrupy.

Beat egg yolks until frothy. Gradually beat in syrup and continue to beat until mixture is thick and pale in color.

Stir in sherry and fold in whipped cream. Spoon into small individual fluted paper cups, sprinkle with ground almonds and freeze for at least 2 hours, or until firm. Serves 8.

9

More Wonderful

Egg Desserts

Here in a second chapter devoted to desserts are creations of textures and flavors that appeal equally to eye and palate. They range from the pristine simplicity of baked meringue shells and puffs of flaky pastry to assembled layers of fragile cake and heavenly creams and custards in such all-time favorites as the Savoy Trifle and the Baked Alaska. None of these glamorous desserts would be possible were it not for eggs.

BAKED ALASKA (Basic Recipe)

We begin with one of the most impressive of all desserts—a cake and ice-cream combination swirled thickly and deeply with a soft meringue and baked in a very hot oven.

3 pints (1½ kilograms) any flavor ice cream or combination of three flavors, partially softened
6 egg whites
½ teaspoon (2 grams) cream of tartar

¾ cup (180 grams) sugar
2 teaspoons (10 milliliters) vanilla essence
1 8- or 9-inch (20- or 22.5-centimeter) round cake layer

Line a 1½-quart (1½-liter) round mixing bowl, 7 to 8 inches (17 to 20 centimeters) across the top with aluminum foil. Press ice cream firmly into bowl and freeze for at least 3 hours or until hard.

Make a 6-egg white Soft Meringue: Beat egg whites and cream of tartar at high speed until foamy. Add sugar, a spoonful at a time, beating constantly until sugar is dissolved* and whites are glossy and stand in soft peaks. Beat in vanilla.

Place cake on an ovenproof serving plate or breadboard covered with aluminum foil. Remove ice cream from bowl and place on the cake, flat side down. Remove foil from ice cream.

Quickly cover all ice cream and cake heavily and completely with meringue. Spread meringue in attractive swirls.

Bake on lowest rack in a preheated 450° F. (230° C.) oven for 5 to 6 minutes. Serves 8 to 10.

For a Baked Alaska to serve 6: Use 1 quart (1 kilogram) ice cream and a meringue made with 4 egg whites, dash of cream of tartar, ½ cup (125 grams) sugar and 1 teaspoon (5 milliliters) vanilla essence.

Orange Alaska

Follow basic preceding recipe but use orange ice or sorbet instead of ice cream. Remove dessert from oven and surround by fresh orange sections or canned mandarin orange sections.

Strawberry Alaska

Follow basic recipe (page 175) but use either vanilla or strawberry ice cream and cover with a thick layer of sliced, chilled and sweetened strawberries. Then cover thickly with meringue and bake.

Cherry Alaska

Cover cake layer (it should be sponge cake for this dessert) with pitted and halved black sweet cherries and sprinkle lightly with a little sugar and some kirsch. Top with raspberry ice or sorbet and cover with meringue. Bake as directed following basic recipe (page 175). Remove dessert from oven, surround by more cherries, sprinkle with heated kirsch and flame at table.

Chocolate Alaska

Follow basic recipe (page 175) but use chocolate ice cream on a chocolate cake base. Coat thickly with meringue into which has been stirred 3 squares

---

* To test if sugar is dissolved, see hint on page oo.

or ounces (90 grams) melted semi-sweet (dark) chocolate. Serve with Hot Chocolate Sauce (page 183).

BAKED ALASKA PIE

1 9-inch (22.5-centimeter) baked Pie Shell (page 159)	6 tablespoons (90 grams) sugar
1 quart (1 kilogram) ice cream	1 teaspoon (5 milliliters) vanilla essence
3 egg whites	Finely granulated or castor sugar
Dash of cream of tartar	

Fill pie shell with ice cream and place in freezer.

Make a 3-egg white Soft Meringue: Beat egg whites with cream of tartar until foamy. Beat in sugar, 1 tablespoon (15 grams) at a time, and continue beating constantly until sugar is dissolved and egg whites are glossy and stand in soft peaks. Stir in vanilla.

Cover ice cream in pie shell with a thick topping of the meringue and sprinkle with finely granulated sugar.

Place pie on an aluminum-covered breadboard and bake in a preheated 475° F. (240° C.) oven for 5 minutes, or until meringue is delicately browned. Serve immediately. Serves 6.

MELON GLACÉ

1 cantaloupe or honeydew melon	1 teaspoon (5 milliliters) vanilla essence
2 egg whites	
Dash cream of tartar	Ice cream
¼ cup (60 grams) sugar	Finely granulated or castor sugar

Cut melon in half and discard seeds. Set melon halves in baking pan filled with crushed ice.

Make a 2-egg white Soft Meringue: Beat egg whites with cream of tartar until foamy. Beat in sugar, 1 tablespoon (15 grams) at a time, and continue beating until meringue is glossy and stands in soft peaks. Stir in vanilla.

Fill melon cavities with ice cream and heap a thick layer of meringue on top. Swirl meringue attractively. Sprinkle lightly with granulated sugar.

Bake in a preheated 475° F. (240° C.) oven for 5 minutes, or until meringue is golden. Serves 2.

MERINGUE SHELLS

4 egg whites

½ teaspoon (2 grams) cream of tartar

1 cup (250 grams) sugar

2 teaspoons (10 milliliters) vanilla
essence

Finely granulated or castor sugar

Ice cream or whipped cream for filling

Fresh berries or sliced fresh fruit for
garnish

Make a 4-egg white Hard Meringue: Beat egg whites with cream of tartar until foamy. Very gradually beat in sugar, a spoonful at a time, and continue to beat at high speed until stiff peaks form. Beat in vanilla.

Line a baking sheet with waxed paper or aluminum foil. Oil paper with fingertips to make sure the entire surface is lightly coated.

With a spoon, drop meringue onto the paper in the shape of half an egg, or spoon meringue into a pastry bag fitted with a large plain tube. Press out the shells to the desired length and width.

Sprinkle shells with finely granulated sugar and bake in a slow 250° F. (120° C.) oven for 30 to 50 minutes, depending upon whether you want them pristine white or delicately browned. Turn off oven and let meringues dry in the warm oven for 1 hour.

To serve, put two together with ice cream or whipped cream in between and serve with fresh berries or sliced fruit, sugared to taste, or a fruit sauce such as Raspberry Sauce au Kirsch (page 171) or English Custard Sauce (page 158). Makes about 16 shells.

MERINGUE NESTS

Make a 4-egg white Hard Meringue (page 178).

Line baking sheet with waxed paper and oil paper lightly. On it outline the desired size and shape of the base of the nests. Base may be circular, heart-shaped or boat-shaped. Fill in base with meringue, then build up a rim around edge of base from 1 to 2 inches (2.5 to 5 centimeters) and about 1-inch (2.5-centimeters) thick. The easiest way to do this is to use a pastry bag fitted with a large plain tube.

Sprinkle nests with finely granulated sugar and bake in a 250° F. (120° C.) for about 30 minutes, watching carefully. When outside is crisp but inside is still a little moist and before they have had a chance to color, remove from oven. With help of a spatula, remove from paper to a cake rack to air-dry and cool. Makes 12 nests.

Note: Hard meringues can be stored in an air-tight container for several weeks. If they lose their crispness, reheat in slow oven for 15 to 20 minutes.

6-EGG WHITE MERINGUE

Follow directions for a 4-egg white Hard Meringue (page 178) using 6 egg whites, 1½ cups (375 grams) sugar in place of the amounts called for in a 4-egg white recipe. Makes 24 shells, 18 nests (depending on size), 3 meringue layers or one crown of meringue called a *vacherin.*

CHOCOLATE MERINGUE

Follow directions for a 4-egg white Hard Meringue (page 178). When soft peaks form, gradually fold in 2 tablespoons (15 grams) cocoa.

PEACH MERINGUE CAKE

4-egg white Hard Meringue (page 178)
2 cups (½ liter) heavy or thick cream, whipped
4 tablespoons (60 grams) sugar
2 cups (500 grams) sliced fresh peaches

Fresh peach for garnish
Shaved Chocolate Curls for garnish (page 163)

Line two baking sheets with waxed paper, oil paper lightly and on each trace two circles 8 inches (20 centimeters) in diameter.

Using a spatula, spread circles thinly with meringue and bake in 250° F. (120° C.) oven for about 20 minutes. Remove circles from the paper with a spatula while they are still white and pliable. They will crisp quickly as they cool.

Set aside one-fourth of the whipped cream. Fold sugar and peaches into remaining whipped cream. Chill.

Just before serving, pile the meringue circles, layer-cake fashion, one atop the other, with a layer of the peaches and cream in between. Spread top with reserved whipped cream and top with peach and Shaved Chocolate Curls. Serves 6.

CHOCOLATE CREAM MERINGUE TORTE

Follow preceding directions for Peach Meringue Cake but put layers together with Chocolate Cream (recipe follows) instead of peaches and cream. Sprinkle top layer of meringue with confectioners or icing sugar and put the torte in the refrigerator "to ripen" for 24 hours.

CHOCOLATE CREAM

2 egg whites
½ cup (125 grams) sugar
1 cup soft (250 grams) unsalted butter

6 ounces (180 grams) sweet (dark) chocolate, melted

In top of double boiler, over hot but not boiling water, beat egg whites until foamy. Gradually beat in sugar, butter and chocolate. Beat well and remove from heat. Continue to beat until cream is cool and thick.

THE SCHAUM TORTE

Two meringue rings mounted on a meringue circle and a wreath of rosettes or "kisses" make one of the most beautiful and festive of all desserts.

Make a 4-egg white Hard Meringue (page 178) twice, using a total of 8 egg whites.

Cover two baking sheets with waxed paper, oil lightly and trace two circles on each sheet, 8 inches (20 centimeters) in diameter and at least 1 inch (2.5 centimeters) apart.

Using a pastry bag fitted with an open-star or plain tube, make a ring around two of the circles about 1-inch (2.5-centimeters) high and thick. Press out a wreath of rosettes or "kisses" around the third circle. To do this, hold the tube vertically over and close to the paper. Squeeze out meringue, raising the tube slowly. Release pressure on bag and draw up and away. The greater the pressure, the larger will be the "kiss."

With a spatula, spread the fourth circle thinly with meringue to make the base of the torte.

Bake the meringues in a slow 250° F. (120° C.) oven for about 30 minutes without letting them color. Remove, while still a little moist, to cake racks to crisp and cool.

Assemble just before serving: Put the fourth circle on a paper doily on a serving plate. Set the two rings on top and fill the container thus made with sweetened whipped cream and sliced fruit or berries, or with whipped cream mixed with chopped brandied fruit or marrons glacés, or with Lime Custard (recipe follows) and top the torte with the wreath of kisses. Serves 8.

LIME CUSTARD

---

4 egg yolks	2 cups (½ liter) heavy or thick cream,
¼ cup (60 milliliters) fresh lime juice	whipped
½ cup (125 grams) sugar	

In large saucepan combine egg yolks, lime juice and sugar. Cook over low heat, stirring constantly, until custard coats the spoon. Be careful not to let it boil.

Cool the custard and fold in the whipped cream. Makes about 1 quart (1 liter).

VACHERIN MERINGUE

Even more impressive than the Schaum Torte is the elaborate crown of meringue known as a *vacherin*.

Make one 4-egg white Hard Meringue (page 178). Make three rings about 1-inch (2.5-centimeters) high and wide and 8 inches (20 centimeters) in diameter on baking sheets lined with lightly oiled waxed paper. Bake in a slow, 250° F. (120° C.) oven for 30 minutes.

While rings are baking, make a second 4-egg white Hard Meringue. Remove the baked rings before they are completely dry. While still moist, mount them one upon the other, sticking them together with a little of the unbaked meringue. Smooth more unbaked meringue around the outside of the rings, as in frosting a cake. Decorate top and sides with scrolls and kisses, wedding-cake fashion, pressing the meringue from a pastry bag fitted with a small open-star tube. Put the decorated crown in the warm oven (heat off) for about 1 hour to dry.

When ready to serve, place *vacherin* on a serving plate lined with doily and fill with fruit and whipped cream or with scoops of a variety of ice creams and sherbets and serve with a fruit sauce. Serves 8.

CREAM PUFFS (Basic Recipe)

¼ cup (60 grams) butter
1 cup (¼ liter) water
1 cup (100 grams) flour
4 large eggs

2 cups (½ liter) filling—ice cream, whipped cream or cream pie custard

Put butter and water in a small saucepan and stir over high heat until butter is melted and liquid is boiling rapidly. Add flour, all at once, raise saucepan a few inches above heat and stir briskly. The paste will come away from sides of pan and form a dough ball in center. Return to heat and cook, stirring, for 30 seconds.

Remove saucepan from heat. Break an egg into the paste and beat vigorously until paste becomes smooth and fluffy. Break in remaining eggs, one at a time, beating vigorously after each addition until paste is smooth and glossy.

Drop paste from a spoon into large mounds 2 inches (5 centimeters) apart on baking sheet. Bake in preheated 375° F. (190° C.) oven for about 50 minutes, or until puffed, golden brown and dry. There should be no beads of moisture on the puffs.

Remove from oven to cool. When cool, split each puff horizontally two-thirds way through and fill with ice cream, whipped cream, sweetened and flavored to taste; or with any of the cream pie fillings. Makes 8 to 10 large puffs.

Miniature Puffs or Profiteroles

Follow preceding Cream Puff basic recipe. Drop paste from a teaspoon into mounds the size of walnuts, 2 inches (5 centimeters) apart on baking sheet. Bake in preheated 375° F. (190° C.) oven for 35 to 50 minutes, or until puffed, well browned and dry. Cool, split and fill. Serve with Hot Chocolate Sauce (recipe follows). Makes 32.

HOT CHOCOLATE SAUCE

8 ounces (250 grams) semi-sweet (dark) chocolate
6 tablespoons (90 milliliters) water

1 teaspoon (grams) instant coffee
1 tablespoon (15 milliliters) Jamaica rum (optional)

In small saucepan combine chocolate, water and coffee. Heat over simmering water or very low heat, stirring until sauce is smooth.

Remove from heat and stir in rum. Serve hot. Makes 1½ cups (375 milliliters).

ÉCLAIRS

Follow basic recipe for Cream Puffs (page 182). Press the paste through a pastry bag fitted with a large round tube into strips about 1 by 4 inches (2.5 by 10 centimeters). Keep the strips 2 inches (5 centimeters) apart on baking sheet. Bake for 50 minutes, or until puffed, nicely brown and dry. Cool, split and fill with sweetened whipped cream or cream custard filling. Brush tops with Hot Chocolate Sauce (see preceding recipe). Makes 10 to 12 éclairs.

PARIS BREST

Make basic Cream Puffs recipe (page 182).

Butter and flour a baking sheet and trace on it a circle 8 to 9 inches (20 to 22.5 centimeters) in diameter. Press out a circle of the cream puff paste about 1-inch (2.5-centimeters) high and 1½-inches (3.5-centimeters) thick through a pastry bag fitted with a large plain tube. Or spoon the paste in mounds around the circle keeping the mounds almost touching.

Bake in a preheated 375° F. (190° C.) oven for 50 to 60 minutes, or until the "crown" is golden brown and dry. Remove from oven to cool. When cool, split carefully crosswise and reassemble with mounds of Chocolate Pastry Cream or Praline Cream between. (Recipes follow.) Decorate all around the sides with large Rosettes of Whipped Cream (page 196) pressed out through a large fluted pastry tube. Serves 6.

CHOCOLATE PASTRY CREAM

2 eggs
2 egg yolks
6 tablespoons (90 grams) sugar
6 tablespoons (36 grams) flour
2 envelopes (15 grams) plain gelatin
12 ounces (375 grams) semi-sweet (dark) chocolate
10 tablespoons (150 milliliters) strong coffee

1½ cups (375 milliliters) hot milk
4 egg whites, stiffly beaten
1 cup (¼ liter) heavy or thick cream, whipped
2 tablespoons (30 milliliters) dark Jamaica rum

In a saucepan beat eggs, egg yolks, sugar and flour until light and fluffy. Stir in gelatin.

In another saucepan cut chocolate into small pieces, add coffee and stir over low heat until chocolate is melted and mixture is smooth. Stir in hot milk, then stir this chocolate milk into the egg mixture. Cook over low heat until cream is hot and thickened. Remove from heat, place in a bowl over cracked ice and stir until mixture is cool.

Fold in egg whites, cream and rum. Makes about 3 cups (¾ liter).

PRALINE CREAM

1 cup (250 grams) sugar
⅓ cup (75 milliliters) water
Dash of cream of tartar
4 egg yolks, beaten
1 cup (250 grams) unsalted butter,
    softened

2 teaspoons (10 milliliters) vanilla
    essence
½ cup (60 grams) Praline Powder
    (recipe follows)

In small saucepan combine sugar, water and cream of tartar. Bring slowly to a boil, then boil rapidly until syrup spins a long thread.

Gradually pour the syrup into egg yolks, beating constantly. Continue to beat until mixture is very thick.

Gradually beat in butter, a little at a time, stir in vanilla and Praline Powder. If too thin, chill until thick.

This is a very rich cream. To use as a filling for Paris Brest, alternate mounds of this Praline Cream with mounds of whipped cream.

Makes about 2 cups (500 grams).

PRALINE POWDER

¾ cup (180 grams) sugar
⅓ cup (75 milliliters) water
Dash of cream of tartar

½ cup (60 grams) finely chopped
    blanched almonds

In heavy saucepan dissolve sugar, water and cream of tartar over low heat. Add almonds and cook, without stirring, until syrup turns a rich amber in color. Watch carefully to see that it does not burn.

Remove immediately from heat and pour syrup into a lightly oiled pan to cool and harden. When hard, remove from pan and pulverize in a mortar with a pestle or in an electric blender. Store in a jar with a tight-fitting lid. Makes ½ cup (125 grams).

CRÊPES SUZETTE

Crepes basic recipe (page 96)
2 tablespoons (30 grams) sugar
¾ cup (180 grams) unsalted butter, softened
1 cup (250 grams) granulated or castor sugar

2 oranges
5 ounces (155 milliliters) curaçao, Cognac or Grand Marnier
6 large lumps sugar
½ cup (125 milliliters) orange juice
⅓ cup (75 milliliters) Grand Marnier

Add sugar to basic crepe batter and make 9 large or 12 small crepes. Set aside.

In a small bowl beat half the butter until light and fluffy. Slowly beat in ¼ cup (60 grams) of the sugar, grated rind of 1 orange and 2 tablespoons (30 milliliters) curaçao, Cognac or Grand Marnier. Spread the pale side of the crepes with this orange butter; fold each in half, then in half again, forming wedge-shaped triangles.

Put the thin slivered rind of the other orange and the sugar lumps, which should be well rubbed over the skin of the orange to absorb its oil or zest, into a chafing dish or electric frying pan with remaining butter, granulated sugar, ½ cup (125 milliliters) orange juice and ½ cup (125 milliliters) of the curaçao, Cognac or Grand Marnier. Bring slowly to a boil, stirring occasionally, until syrupy. Add the skinned sections of remaining oranges.

Place the stuffed crepes in the hot sauce, spooning it over them to coat evenly. Warm the Grand Marnier, ignite it and pour flaming over the crepes. Shake the pan until flame dies out. Serve on warm plates. Serves 6.

CRÊPES TRIOMPHANTES

Crepes basic recipe (page 96)
2 tablespoons (30 grams) sugar
1 tablespoon (15 milliliters) Cognac
Milk, if necessary
1 small orange
4 tablespoons (60 grams) butter
6 tablespoons (90 grams) sugar

½ cup (125 milliliters) Cognac
2 ounces or squares (60 grams) bitter chocolate
Vanilla ice cream
Hot Chocolate Sauce (page 183)
Toasted slivered almonds

Make crepe batter, adding the 2 tablespoons sugar. If it becomes thicker than heavy cream upon standing, stir in the tablespoon of Cognac, and thin it, if necessary, with a little milk. Make crepes. You will need only eight for this recipe. Refrigerate or freeze the rest (page 96).

Cut rind from the orange in one continuous piece, just as in peeling an apple. Cut orange flesh in half and set aside.

In frying pan melt butter. Add sugar and the spiral of orange peel and cook over medium heat, stirring constantly, until mixture caramelizes to a dark brown color.

Using the peeled orange, immediately squeeze in about 2 tablespoons (30 millileters) orange juice to prevent further caramelization. Add Cognac, stir and set aflame. As soon as flame dies out, discard orange rind and add the chocolate. Cook, stirring, until chocolate is melted and sauce is smooth.

Put a large spoonful of vanilla ice cream on lower third of each crepe, and roll the crepes into cylinders.

Place one crepe on each serving plate, cover with chocolate sauce, and sprinkle with almonds. Serves 8.

ZABAGLIONE OR SABAYON SAUCE

4 egg yolks
¼ cup (60 grams) finely granulated or
   castor sugar

⅔ cup (150 milliliters) Marsala,
   sherry or Madeira wine

Beat egg yolks and gradually add, still beating, the sugar and wine. Place mixture over boiling water and whisk until custard foams up in pan and begins to thicken. Do not overcook; it should be the consistency of soap suds. Spoon into sherbet glasses and serve warm with a sweet crisp cookie or biscuit, or use as a sauce over sweet crepes. Serves 4.

LUSCIOUS CHOCOLATE CAKE

¾ cup (180 grams) butter, softened
2 cups (500 grams) sugar
3 eggs
3 cups (300 grams) flour
1½ teaspoons baking or bicarbonate
   soda (7 grams)
1½ cups (375 milliliters) buttermilk
1 teaspoon (5 milliliters) vanilla
   essence

1½ teaspoons (7 milliliters) lemon
   juice
3 squares or ounces (90 grams) unsweetened chocolate, melted
½ cup (60 grams) chopped nuts, optional

Oil three 8-inch (20-centimeter) layer-cake tins or one 13 x 9 x 2-inch (32 x 22 x 5-centimeter) oblong cake tin. Line with waxed paper and oil the paper.

In mixing bowl cream butter and sugar until light. Beat in eggs, one at a time, beating well after each addition. Set aside.

Combine flour and baking soda. Add dry ingredients to egg mixture alternately with the buttermilk, stirring well after each addition until batter is smooth. Stir in vanilla, lemon juice, melted chocolate and nuts.

Pour batter into oblong tin or divide evenly among the layer-cake tins. Bake in preheated 350° F. (180° C.) oven: layers for 30 to 35 minutes; oblong for 45 minutes, or until cake tests done.

Remove cake from oven, let cool 5 minutes, then run knife around edge of cake and turn out onto wire rack.

When cake is completely cool, put layers together with Chocolate-Mocha Butter Cream; frost top and sides lavishly with Meringue Frosting. (Recipes follow.) Or, spread oblong cake thickly with Chocolate-Mocha Butter Cream. Serves 10 to 12.

CHOCOLATE-MOCHA BUTTER CREAM

6 ounces (180 grams) semi-sweet
   (dark) chocolate pieces
¼ cup (60 milliliters) hot water or
   strong coffee
4 egg yolks (reserve white for Meringue Frosting)

1 tablespoon (15 milliliters) vanilla
   essence or dark rum
½ cup (125 grams) soft butter

In small-sized saucepan over low heat melt chocolate in water or coffee. Remove from heat and beat in egg yolks and vanilla or rum. Gradually beat in butter, bit by bit. If butter cream is too soft, chill for 1 hour before using.

To make in an electric blender: Put chocolate into blender. Cover and grate on high speed. Add hot water or coffee and blend for 20 seconds or until smooth. With motor on, drop in egg yolks one by one. Drop in butter and add vanilla while blending. If necessary, stop motor and stir down butter-cream a couple of times until smooth. Makes about 2 cups (500 grams).

MERINGUE FROSTING
OR ITALIAN MERINGUE

1½ cups (375 grams) sugar
½ cup (125 milliliters) water
1 teaspoon (5 milliliters) lemon juice
    or ½ teaspoon (2 grams) cream
    of tartar

4 egg whites
2 teaspoons (10 milliliters) vanilla
    essence

In saucepan combine sugar, water and lemon juice or cream of tartar. Bring to a boil over low heat, then boil rapidly until bubbles get thick and syrup spins a thread when a little is dripped from tines of a fork (238° F. or 115° C. on a candy thermometer).

Beat egg whites in a large bowl until thick and glossy. Gradually beat in the hot syrup and continue to beat until frosting is thick enough to hold its shape. Beat in vanilla. If possible, use an electric mixer unless you have a very strong arm!

LADY BALTIMORE CAKE

This is the perfect way to use many leftover egg whites.

1 cup (250 grams) butter, softened
2 cups (500 grams) sugar
3 cups (300 grams) sifted flour
6 teaspoons (30 grams) baking powder
1 cup (¼ liter) milk

7 egg whites
1 teaspoon (5 milliliters) vanilla
    essence
Lady Baltimore Cake Frosting (recipe
    follows)

Oil three 8-inch (20-centimeter) layer-cake tins and line with waxed paper. Oil waxed paper.

In mixing bowl cream together butter and sugar until light and fluffy.

Combine dry ingredients and stir into butter mixture alternately with the milk.

Beat egg whites until stiff enough to hold a peak and fold gently but thoroughly into batter. Fold in vanilla.

Divide batter into prepared cake tins and bake in a preheated 350° F. (180° C.) oven for 25 to 30 minutes, or until layers test done. Cool for 5 minutes, then turn layers out onto cake racks to cool completely.

When cool, fill and frost with Lady Baltimore Cake Frosting. Serves 8 to 10.

LADY BALTIMORE CAKE FROSTING

Make 4–egg white Meringue Frosting (page 189). Fold in 1 cup (125 grams) chopped nuts, ⅓ cup (40 grams) chopped seedless raisins or sultanas and ½ cup (60 grams) each chopped candied cherries and diced candied pineapple.

GÉNOISE (Basic Recipe)

This is one of the most delicate cakes in the world. It is the base of many *gâteaux*, those beautiful French cakes thàt one sees on the dessert table of French restaurants. It is not difficult to make if directions are carefully followed.

½ cup (125 grams) unsalted butter	1 teaspoon (5 milliliters) vanilla
6 eggs	essence
1 cup (250 grams) sugar	1 cup (100 grams) flour, sifted

To make Clarified Butter which you will need in this recipe: Melt butter over low heat. Spoon off any froth from surface and set butter aside to cool to lukewarm.

Oil a 9-inch (22.5-centimeter) layer-cake tin that is about 2 inches (5 centimeters) deep. Line bottom with waxed paper and oil paper.

Put eggs (in their shells) into a saucepan of rather hot water for 5 minutes. Rinse mixing bowl with hot water and dry thoroughly. Use an electric mixer if possible.

Break warm eggs into the warm bowl. Add sugar. Beat at high speed for 10 minutes, or until mixture is very thick and takes some time to level out when beater is withdrawn. This is known as a "ribbon" stage.

Add vanilla. Add the flour by sifting a little at a time over the batter and gently folding it in by hand. This is the best way to make a successful Génoise. Turn batter over and over from top to bottom until all flour is slowly incorporated. Still using your hand, gently fold in lukewarm Clarified Butter, being careful not to include any of the sediment that has settled to the bottom of the pan.

Turn batter into prepared tin and bake in a preheated 325° F. (170° C.) oven for about 40 minutes, or until cake leaves side of tin and cake tester inserted in center comes out clean. Run a spatula around edge of cake to loosen it from sides of tin and carefully turn out cake onto a rack to cool. When cool, split, fill and frost as desired. The easiest way to split the cake layer in half horizontally is to mark half the width all the way around with an occasional toothpick, then place a length of strong thread around it and gently pull it through the cake. Serves 8.

Génoise is especially delicious with Lemon Butter Filling and iced with Lemon Frosting.

Lemon Butter Filling

¼ cup (60 grams) butter
1 cup (250 grams) sugar
6 egg yolks
1 teaspoon (2 grams) grated lemon
    rind

6 tablespoons (90 milliliters) lemon
    juice

Combine all ingredients in top of double boiler. Cook over simmering water, stirring frequently, for 10 to 20 minutes, or until smooth and thickened. Cool quickly. Makes 1½ cups (375 grams).

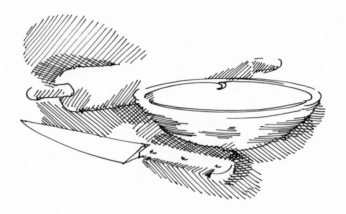

Lemon Frosting

4 egg yolks
¼ cup (60 grams) finely granulated or
    castor sugar
1 tablespoon (8 grams) grated lemon
    rind

3 tablespoons (45 milliliters) lemon
    juice
3 cups (750 grams) confectioners or
    icing sugar

In heavy saucepan combine egg yolks, granulated sugar, lemon rind and juice. Cook over low heat, stirring rapidly, until mixture is smooth and thickened throughout. Do not let it boil. Remove from heat and gradually beat in confectioners sugar. Makes enough icing to cover a 9-inch (22.5-centimeter) layer cake.

JELLY OR JAM ROLL

---

5 large eggs, separated
4 tablespoons (60 grams) sugar
3 tablespoons (18 grams) flour, sifted
2 teaspoons (10 milliliters) vanilla
essence

Finely granulated or castor sugar
3 tablespoons (45 grams) red currant
jelly or jam

Oil an 18 x 12-inch (45 x 30-centimeter) Swiss-roll tin or jelly-roll pan. Line with waxed paper and oil paper thoroughly. The best way to do this is with the fingertips.

Beat egg yolks and sugar until thick and pale in color. Use an electric mixer, if possible. Carefully fold in flour and vanilla.

Beat egg whites until soft peaks form when beater is withdrawn and fold into cake batter. Spread batter evenly and well into the corners of the prepared pan.

Bake in a preheated 350° F. (180° C.) oven for 12 minutes.

Remove cake from oven and loosen paper from sides of pan. Sprinkle surface with a little granulated sugar and turn out onto a sheet of waxed paper. Remove waxed paper from bottom of cake, sprinkle with granulated sugar and spread with jelly or jam. Roll lengthwise into a long thin roll.

Slice and serve as a delicate and delicious tea cake, dessert or use to line the bowl in making a Savoy Trifle (page 197). Serves 8.

ROULADE AU CHOCOLAT (Chocolate Roll)

As light as a breath of spring air, the Roulade au Chocolat contains no flour. Actually it is a chocolate soufflé, baked in a jelly-roll pan, and allowed to deflate before being filled with whipped cream and rolled.

6 ounces (180 grams) semi-sweet
    (dark) chocolate
1 teaspoon (2 grams) instant coffee
3 tablespoons (45 milliliters) hot water
6 eggs, separated
⅔ cups (150 grams) sugar
Cocoa (not a cocoa mix)

1½ cups (375 milliliters) heavy or
    thick cream
2 tablespoons (30 grams) confection-
    ers or icing sugar
2 teaspoons (10 milliliters) vanilla
    essence

Oil a 14 x 10-inch (35 x 25-centimeter) Swiss-roll tin or jelly-roll pan. Line with waxed paper and oil paper.

In small saucepan stir chocolate over low heat with coffee and water until chocolate is melted and mixture is smooth. Set aside to cool.

Meanwhile, beat egg yolks and sugar—with an electric mixer if possible—at high speed for at least 5 minutes, or until mixture is pale in color and as thick as a cake batter. It should take some time to level out when beater is withdrawn.

Stir in cooled chocolate.

Beat egg whites with a clean beater until glossy and thick enough to hold a soft peak. Pour the chocolate mixture on top of egg whites and fold in, cutting down through the mixture with the edge of a large kitchen spoon, until whites are thoroughly incorporated into the chocolate mixture.

Pour batter onto prepared baking sheet and spread evenly and well into the corners of the pan.

Bake in center of a preheated 350° F. (180° C.) oven for 15 minutes. Do not overbake.

Remove baking sheet from oven, cover top of cake with a sheet of waxed paper, cover waxed paper with a kitchen or tea towel and let cool for 1 hour.

Remove towel and waxed paper. The cake will look depleted and very sad, but take heart—it won't taste that way! Run a knife around edge of pan to loosen cake. Overlap two strips of waxed paper lengthwise on worktable. They should be wider than width of the cake. Sift cocoa over surface of cake to coat it generously, then flip baking sheet and cake upside down onto center of the paper strips. The long side of the baking sheet should be horizontal to you.

Remove baking sheet: Grasp edge of waxed paper lining the sheet and gently raise baking sheet from right to left. Remove waxed paper from bottom of cake. If you oiled the paper well, you'll have no trouble, but if you didn't, or if you left any little lumps of egg whites in the batter, you may find the cake will stick in spots. Free these spots with a knife.

Beat cream until stiff, then beat in confectioners sugar and vanilla. With spatula, spread cream in an even layer over surface of the cake.

Using both hands, grasp the wide side of the waxed paper closest to you on the table, raise the edge of the cake and flip about 1 inch (2.5 centimeters) over on top of the filling. Continue to lift the waxed paper and roll cake and filling, making a long roll about 4 inches (10 centimeters) in diameter. Don't be upset if the cake cracks a little, especially on your first try. It usually does.

The last roll of the cake should deposit the "log" well into the center of the back sheet of waxed paper.

Place a serving platter or board on the far side of the roll, parallel to it, and lift waxed paper and roll onto the board. I usually leave the waxed paper under the roll until I am ready to serve the dessert. Chill.

When ready to serve, sift a little more cocoa over the surface of the roll and cut away all visible waxed paper with a sharp knife, leaving a small strip under the roll. Discard the paper as the cake is served. Slice thickly on a slight diagonal. Serves 8 to 10.

TIPSY PUDDING

---

1 9-inch (22.5-centimeter) layer cake, sponge or Génoise
12 egg yolks
1 cup (250 grams) sugar
¾ cup (75 grams) flour
4 cups (1 liter) hot milk
2 cups (½ liter) heavy or thick cream, hot
2 teaspoons (10 milliliters) vanilla essence

¾ cup (180 milliliters) rum or Madeira wine
2 cups (½ liter) heavy or thick cream for whipping
½ cup (125 grams) confectioners or icing sugar
Rosettes of Whipped Cream (page 196)
Toasted slivered almonds

Slice cake into three layers horizontally. For easiest method see page 191.

In large saucepan beat egg yolks, sugar and flour. Gradually stir in hot milk and hot cream. Cook over moderate heat, stirring constantly and rapidly with a wooden spoon, making sure spoon reaches all parts of sides and bottom of pan. Do not boil. When custard is smooth and thick, remove from heat and stir in 1 teaspoon (5 milliliters) of the vanilla. Cool.

Place a cake layer in bottom of a large glass serving dish. Sprinkle with ¼ cup (60 milliliters) rum or Madeira and cover with half the custard. Place second layer of cake over custard, sprinkle with another ¼ cup (60 milliliters) rum or Madeira and cover with remaining custard. Top with remaining slice of cake, sprinkle with remaining rum or Madeira and chill.

Before serving, whip cream until thick and stir in confectioners sugar and remaining teaspoon vanilla. Cover top of cake with large "kisses" or Rosettes of Whipped Cream (page 196) and garnish with almonds. Serves 12.

ROSETTES OF WHIPPED CREAM

When whipped cream is to be used for decorative rosettes, whipped the cream in a blender and blend only 1 cup (¼ liter) at a time for best results. As soon as cream begins to thicken, turn off blender and stir cream with a rubber spatula; repeat several times until cream is very thick. The cream will not have the volume that it would have if beaten with a rotary beater or a wire whisk, but the plus factor is that it does not "weep." Rosettes made by this method also freeze beautifully. Just pipe rosettes with a pastry tube onto a baking sheet lined with waxed paper and put in freezer. When solid, remove rosettes and drop into a freezer bag. Use as needed. Will remain fresh and ready to use for at least a month.

SAVOY TRIFLE

1 Jelly or Jam Roll (page 193)
1 envelope (8 grams) plain gelatin
¼ cup (60 milliliters) cold water
2 cups (½ liter) hot milk
¾ cup (180 grams) sugar
4 egg yolks, beaten
2 ounces (60 milliliters) dark Jamaica
    rum

1 cup (¼ liter) heavy or thick cream,
    whipped
¼ cup (60 milliliters) sherry
Rosettes of Whipped Cream (page
    196), optional

In saucepan soak gelatin in water for 5 minutes. Add hot milk and sugar and cook over low heat until mixture is very hot, but not boiling. Pour the hot milk gradually over beaten egg yolks, beating constantly. Stir in rum and stir over a bowl of cracked ice until cream is cool and beginning to set. Fold in whipped cream.

Slice jelly roll thinly. Use two-thirds of the slices to line bottom and sides of a glass serving dish. Sprinkle slices with sherry and pour in the rum-cream. Top with remaining slices and chill until set. If desired, garnish with rosettes of additional whipped cream before serving. Serves 6.

IO

An Assortment
of Egg Sauces
and Dressings

Our friend the versatile and helpful egg forms the basis of so many of our favorite sauces and salad dressings. This last chapter offers an assortment—some of which are necessary ingredients in other recipes in the book—all of which, it is hoped, will bring you greater eating pleasure.

MEDIUM CREAM SAUCE (Basic Recipe)

3 tablespoons (45 grams) butter
3 tablespoons (18 grams) flour
1 cup (¼ liter) hot milk
½ teaspoon (1 gram) salt, or to taste

Dash white pepper
½ cup (125 milliliters) heavy or thick
  cream

In saucepan melt butter. Stir in flour and cook over low heat, stirring, for 2 minutes, or until butter-flour mixture is bubbling.

Remove saucepan from heat. Add milk, all at once, and stir vigorously with a wooden spoon or wire whisk until sauce is smooth. Return to moderate heat and cook, stirring or whisking until sauce is thickened. Stir in salt and pepper and cream. Makes about 1 cup (¼ liter).

LIGHT CREAM SAUCE

Make as above but use only 2 tablespoons (30 grams) butter and 2 table-spoons (12 grams) flour.

HEAVY CREAM SAUCE

Make as above but use 4 tablespoons (60 grams) butter and 4 tablespoons (24 grams) flour.

BASIC WHITE SAUCE (Béchamel Sauce)

3 tablespoons (45 grams) butter	1 small onion, sliced
3 tablespoons (18 grams) flour	½ teaspoon (1 gram) salt, or to taste
2 cups (½ liter) hot milk	Dash white pepper

In saucepan melt butter over low heat. When melted, add flour and stir until butter and flour are well blended and beginning to bubble.

Remove saucepan from heat. Add hot milk, all at once, the onion and salt and pepper. Return saucepan to moderate heat and cook, stirring vigorously from bottom and sides of pan, until sauce is smooth and thickened.

Reduce heat to very low and cook sauce for a few minutes, stirring occasionally. Discard onion slices. Makes about 2 cups (½ liter).

MORNAY SAUCE

2 cups (½ liter) milk	½ cup (125 milliliters) heavy or thick
1 bay leaf	cream
1 slice medium onion	Pinch dry mustard
¼ teaspoon (or 6) peppercorns	3 tablespoons (25 grams) grated Par-
6 tablespoons (90 grams) butter	mesan cheese
6 tablespoons (36 grams) flour	1 tablespoon (8 grams) shredded
Dash of salt and cayenne	Gruyère or Swiss cheese

In small saucepan heat milk with bay leaf, onion slice and peppercorns until steaming.

In larger saucepan melt 4 tablespoons (60 grams) of the butter. Stir in flour, the salt and cayenne and cook, stirring, until mixture is smooth and begins to bubble. Remove from heat and strain the hot milk into the butter-flour mixture or roux. Return to heat and bring to a boil, stirring vigorously.

When sauce is smooth and thickened, stir in the remaining butter, bit by bit, then add cream, mustard, and the cheeses. Keep sauce hot over low heat for 5 to 10 minutes. Makes about 2½ cups (625 milliliters).

SWISS CHEESE SAUCE

2 tablespoons (30 grams) butter
2 tablespoons (12 grams) flour
Dash of salt
1 cup (¼ liter) milk

1 cup (125 grams) shredded Swiss
    cheese
Freshly ground white pepper to taste

In a small saucepan melt butter. Stir in flour and salt. Cook over low heat, stirring constantly, until barely bubbling. Gradually stir in milk and cook over low heat, stirring constantly, until sauce is smooth and thickened. Cook, stirring, for 1 minute.

Remove sauce from heat and stir in cheese little by little until melted and smooth. Stir in freshly ground pepper to taste. Cover and keep warm until ready to use. Makes about 2 cups (½ liter).

MUSHROOM SAUCE

½ pound (250 grams) mushrooms,
    chopped
2 tablespoons (30 grams) butter
1 cup (250 milliliters) Basic White
    Sauce or Medium Cream Sauce
    (page 200 and 199)

¼ cup (60 milliliters) cream
Salt and white pepper to taste

Sauté mushrooms in butter for about 5 minutes or until soft. Add Basic White Sauce or Medium Cream Sauce and cook for 10 minutes, stirring occasionally.

Stir in cream and correct seasoning with salt and pepper. Makes about 2 cups (½ liter).

MUSHROOM DUXELLES

1½ pounds (750 grams) mushrooms, finely chopped
6 scallions or spring onions, minced
½ cup (125 grams) butter

¼ cup (60 milliliters) Madeira wine
2 tablespoons (15 grams) chopped parsley
Freshly ground white pepper

In a large frying pan sauté mushrooms and scallions in butter over moderately high heat until mushrooms give up most of their liquid and become dry. Add Madeira, parsley and pepper and continue to cook until wine is almost completely reduced and mixture has no excess liquid. Makes 1½ cups (375 milliliters).

MADEIRA SAUCE (Sauce Madère)

1 tablespoon (15 grams) butter
4 large mushrooms, sliced
2 tablespoons (15 grams) finely chopped shallots or sweet onion

Salt and freshly ground pepper
⅓ cup (75 milliliters) Madeira wine
1½ cups (375 milliliters) brown sauce or gravy, homemade or canned

In frying pan heat butter and sauté mushrooms over low heat for about 5 minutes. Add shallots or sweet onion and cook, stirring, until most of the liquid from the mushrooms has evaporated. Sprinkle with salt and pepper.

Add wine and cook over moderate heat for 1 minute. Add brown sauce or gravy and simmer for 15 minutes. Makes about 2 cups (½ liter).

SHERRY MUSTARD SAUCE

1 egg
¼ cup (60 milliliters) sherry
¼ cup (60 milliliters) vinegar
2 tablespoons (30 grams) sugar

1½ tablespoons (2 grams) dry
    mustard
1 tablespoon (15 grams) butter
Salt to taste

Put all ingredients into blender container or small mixing bowl. Blend or mix with electric or rotary beater at medium speed until well blended.

Pour into a small saucepan and cook over medium heat, stirring constantly, just until sauce bubbles around the edge and is thick enough to coat the spoon. Remove from heat. Makes about ¾ cup (180 milliliters). This is a wonderful sauce for ham and eggs.

Note: Any remaining sauce will keep well for several weeks in a tightly closed container in the refrigerator.

TOMATO SAUCE

1 cup (250 grams) strained tomatoes
    or tomato puree
1 small onion, chopped
1 bay leaf

Salt to taste
1 tablespoon (6 grams) flour
1 tablespoon (15 grams) butter

In saucepan combine tomatoes or tomato puree, onion, bay leaf and salt. Bring to a boil and simmer for 3 minutes.

Mix flour and butter to a smooth paste. Stir paste into the tomato mixture, bit by bit, and simmer for 10 minutes. Strain before serving. Makes about 1 cup (¼ liter). Excellent on scrambled eggs and plain omelets.

CRAIG'S TOMATO SAUCE

2 tablespoons (30 milliliters) vegetable
  oil
½ cup (60 grams) finely chopped
  onion
1 teaspoon (2 grams) finely minced
  garlic
Dash each dried basil and thyme
¼ cup (60 grams) tomato paste

1 teaspoon (2 grams) flour
1 cup (¼ liter) chicken broth, fresh or
  canned
1 cup (250 grams) chopped canned
  tomatoes
Salt and freshly ground pepper to
  taste
1 tablespoon (15 grams) butter

In saucepan heat oil and sauté onion and garlic for about 3 minutes or until onion is transparent. Add herbs and tomato paste and cook, stirring, about 1 minute. Stir in flour.

Add chicken broth gradually and cook, stirring constantly, until sauce is smooth and thickened. Add tomatoes, salt and pepper and cook, partially covered, for about 15 minutes.

Press sauce through a sieve or food mill. Return to heat, add butter and swirl pan over the heat until butter is just melted. Makes about 2 cups (½ liter). This is a tasty sauce to spoon on scrambled eggs and plain omelets.

SAUCE POLONAISE

¼ cup (60 grams) butter
2 tablespoons (15 grams) chopped
  parsley
1 tablespoon (15 milliliters) lemon
  juice
1½ teaspoons (3 grams) minced
  onion

Salt and freshly ground pepper to
  taste
2 tablespoons (15 grams) fine, dry
  bread crumbs
2 Hard-Boiled Egg yolks (page 16),
  finely chopped or sieved.

In saucepan melt butter over medium heat. Stir in parsley, lemon juice, onion, salt and pepper. Cook, stirring constantly, until onion is transparent, about 2 minutes. Stir in bread crumbs and egg yolks. Makes ½ cup (125 milliliters).

This sauce is particularly good with fish and vegetable dishes.

HOLLANDAISE SAUCE

4 egg yolks

2 tablespoons (30 milliliters) light
   cream

1 tablespoon (15 milliliters) lemon
   juice

½ teaspoon (1 gram) salt

Pinch cayenne pepper

1 cup or ½ pound (250 grams) butter

Into a small bowl put egg yolks, cream, lemon juice, salt and cayenne. Set bowl in a fry pan containing hot water and beat the egg mixture over low heat until it begins to thicken. The water should not boil, barely simmer. Use a wire whisk if possible, otherwise beat with two forks held in one hand.

Beat in the butter, bit by bit. When all butter has been added, turn off heat and pour a little cold water into the water in the skillet to reduce temperature and prevent further cooking of the sauce. It will stay warm for 10 to 15 minutes. Makes 1½ cups (375 milliliters).

Hollandaise Sauce is delicious on many different egg dishes, on fresh vegetables and on different kinds of poached fish.

MOUSSELINE SAUCE

Add 2 heaping tablespoons (30 grams) of stiffly whipped cream to a cup of Hollandaise Sauce (see preceding recipe). Heat the sauce carefully in a bowl placed in hot water in a frying pan and whip gently until hot. Do not let the water boil or the sauce will curdle.

The uses for Mousseline Sauce are the same as those for Hollandaise Sauce.

AURORA SAUCE

Make 1½ cups (375 milliliters) Hollandaise Sauce (page 205). Let cool. Add and blend in, stirring down occasionally with a rubber spatula if necessary, ½ cup (125 grams) Mayonnaise (page 207) and ½ cup (125 milliliters) heavy or thick cream. Makes 2½ cups (625 milliliters).

Sauce Aurora is delightful on Eggs in Aspic (page 120) and is a nice accompaniment to cold savory mousses as well.

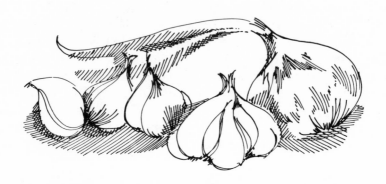

BÉARNAISE SAUCE

2 spring onions or shallots, chopped
Dash of dried tarragon
6 peppercorns
¼ cup (60 milliliters) white wine
¼ cup (60 milliliters) tarragon vinegar
3 egg yolks

1 tablespoon (15 milliliters) water
1 cup or ½ pound (250 grams) unsalted butter
½ teaspoon (1 gram) salt
Dash cayenne pepper

In saucepan combine onions or shallots, tarragon, peppercorns, white wine and vinegar. Bring to a boil and boil rapidly until most of the liquid has evaporated.

Remove saucepan from heat and stir in egg yolks, which have been lightly beaten with the water. Place saucepan into a frying pan of simmering water and add butter bit by bit, whisking or stirring continually. The beating should not be too fast, but should be steady and constant until sauce is as thick as mayonnaise. Stir in salt and cayenne. Makes about 1½ cups (375 milliliters).

Béarnaise Sauce adds zest to broiled and grilled meats and fish.

MAYONNAISE (Blender Method)

This is a foolproof blender recipe. Don't try to double it. It won't work!

1 egg

2 tablespoons (30 milliliters) lemon
   juice or vinegar

½ teaspoon (1 gram) salt

Dash of dry mustard

Dash cayenne or freshly ground white
   pepper

1 cup (¼ liter) salad or vegetable oil
   (part olive oil is always good)

Into blender container break the egg. Add lemon juice or vinegar, salt, mustard, cayenne or white pepper and ¼ cup (60 milliliters) of the oil.

Cover container and begin blending on low speed. With motor on, remove cover and immediately add remaining oil in a heavy stream. Makes 1¼ cups (310 milliliters).

Or, try some other tasty variations. . . .

Garlic Mayonnaise

Add to ingredients in container 1 large clove garlic, peeled and split.

Herb Mayonnaise

Add 1 tablespoon (8 grams) fresh chopped herbs or a dash of dried.

Parsley Mayonnaise

When mayonnaise is made, add 1 tablespoon (8 grams) of parsley, stir, and blend for 10 seconds longer.

Caper Mayonnaise

When mayonnaise is made, add 1 tablespoon (8 grams) well-drained capers. Stir and blend for 10 seconds longer.

Watercress Mayonnaise

Combine 1 cup (¼ liter) mayonnaise with ½ cup (60 grams) finely chopped watercress, 1 tablespoon (15 milliliters) lemon juice, a good dash of dry mustard and salt to taste.

Sauce Andalouse

Combine 2 cups (½ liter) mayonnaise with 2 tablespoons (30 grams) to-mato ketchup and 2 tablespoons (15 grams) finely chopped pimento.

FRENCH DRESSING (Vinaigrette Sauce)

---

1 clove garlic, peeled and split
½ teaspoon (1 gram) salt
Freshly ground black pepper to taste
Dash dry mustard or 1 teaspoon (5 grams) prepared Dijon-type

1 tablespoon (15 milliliters) vinegar or fresh lemon juice
3 to 4 tablespoons (45 to 60 milliliters) salad oil, or to taste

Put garlic and salt into a small mixing bowl. Mash and bruise garlic lightly in the salt with back of a spoon or a pestle. Add pepper, mustard and vinegar or lemon juice and whip thoroughly with a fork until spices are blended. Discard garlic clove.

Gradually whip or whisk oil into the blended spices. Set aside until ready to use. Whisk again lightly before using in a recipe or pouring over salad greens.

Makes about ¼ cup (60 milliliters), or enough to dress a salad to serve 4. You may double recipe. This dressing is good on all green and vegetable salads.

MIMOSA DRESSING

Sieve the yolk of one Hard-Boiled Egg (page 16), and add to French Dressing just before serving. Mimosa makes a most decorative dressing for greens.

LOUIS DRESSING

---

1 cup (250 grams) Mayonnaise (page 207)
¼ cup (60 grams) chili sauce
1 Hard-Boiled Egg (page 16), finely chopped

2 tablespoons (15 grams) finely chopped ripe olives
1 tablespoon (8 grams) minced chives
1 tablespoon (15 milliliters) lemon juice

Combine all ingredients. Mix well and chill. Makes 1½ cups (375 milliliters). Egg Salad Louis (page 72) is traditionally dressed with this dressing.

Index